Mermaid
Our Family in Paradise

Philip Rink

Please visit us at www.caribmermaid.com.
You may enjoy our companion video.

Copyright 2003 by Phil Rink.
Published by:
PRPR LLC
P.O. Box 729
Stanwood, WA, 98292
www.caribmermaid.com

ISBN 0-9727906-1-6.

Contents

Dedication

To my wife and partner Nancy. The beauty and wisdom of our children is a reflection of their mother.

Acknowledgements:

Thank you Jackie Pels from Hardscratch Press for editing this stuff.

Thanks to John Rink (my Dad), Char Thomas and Barb Wakelee for saving our emails and giving me copies when we got home.

Thanks to David Darwent and Bruce Shattenburg for the advice and encouragement that saved us from our original plans and set us on the correct path.

Note about the book:

The emails in this book were written during our adventure and were send to our mailing list of approximately 110 families. They are reproduced with as little editing as possible.

The text between the emails has been edited as throughly as we can stand. The apparent mistakes still present have been left to make the writing more colorful and add interest. I hope you enjoy them.

-Phil Rink

Leaving the Lagoon

On the second Wednesday in November we woke at dawn and had a light breakfast. For the first day since beginning the trip two weeks earlier, the kids didn't start their day with school-work. Most of our gear and supplies had already been stowed under the seats and beds, in lockers, and in Mermaid's various nooks and crannies. Some of our supplies were still piled under the table in the main cabin. My "to do" list was down to two pages, mostly minor repairs and maintenance.

At about 8:30 I started the diesel engine and let it warm. Its rough idle soon settled into a smooth, loud rumble from be-tween the kids' aft cabins. I slipped the transmission into forward and advanced the throttle slightly, powering the boat into the calm breeze of the anchorage. On the bow, Nancy used the electric windlass to retrieve the anchor chain as it came slack. The windlass brought the anchor up into the bow roller and she tied it off with a nylon-line snubber.

Lena and Pender, 12 and 9, were in the cabin, putting breakfast away and stowing anything loose. We motored slowly through the uncrowded anchorage, waving at people sipping coffee on deck, going to work in their dinghies, or preparing their own boats to travel.

The drawbridge from the south end of St. Maarten's central lagoon opens at 9 a.m. for outbound boat traffic, and we were early. Several other boats were also ready for the opening, and they circled with us or lazily drifted nearby. The kids finished below and came on deck. Their skin was already starting to tan, and their dark blond hair was glowing with highlights.

The bridge opened at 9:05 and we were third in line as the boats queued up. I advanced the throttle and motored through the cut at six knots, surprised at the light currents and easy steering in the narrow channel. Suddenly, without any particu-lar ceremony, our family of four was sailing our own boat in the Caribbean Sea.

Phil, Pender, Nancy and Lena. Sandy Spit, BVI.

Background

I am an engineer. My father, who is also an engineer, grew up on a farm in north-central Indiana. My uncles and cousins still farm there, growing wheat, soybeans, feed corn, and beef cattle.

About 10 years ago I was developing assembly-line equipment for a U.S. auto manufacturer. We shipped a prototype to a plant just south of Detroit, then my boss and I went out to watch the equipment work and discuss what to do next. We wanted to see our equipment in use, see the general factory conditions, and meet with the people who would use and maintain our equipment so that we could make sure we accommodated their concerns. Our machine packaged delicate components, protecting them until they were needed, then presenting them to the workers one at a time for installation into a complex assembly. It worked great and was well-received in the factory. In a design review later in the week, though, we heard a different story.

A stern, middle-aged man in an expensive suit informed us that our design and construction was too flimsy.

"Nonsense," I said in my politically savvy way, "this thing never breaks down, and the components and design are incredibly simple and reliable. It's nowhere near as complex and big as most of the equipment you have on the floor, and the smaller-size components mean that the structure can also be smaller."

"Look, I can stick a screwdriver in right here and break the whole thing, and you'll have to replace this drive gear and belt," the suit says.

"Well, you're right," I answer. "If you want to break the thing, you can. I'm not sure I can make it sabotage-proof."

"If you want to be in the automotive industry, that's what you need to do."

The next day, Friday, I talked to the people working the assembly line. They all had stories of people wanting a break and sabotaging the line, just because they were mad at their boss, or too cold, or too hot, or too short, or too fat, or too bald. "Yeah, but after they were fired, things must have settled down, right?" "No one gets fired." "Oh."

Saturday morning I got up early, ate my 10 dollar expense account breakfast and drank my four dollar expense account orange juice, then changed into overalls and a tee-shirt and drove to see my relatives in Indiana. I got to the farms in mid-morning. My Uncle Pete, who I hadn't seen for years, was just starting to mow hay. He had made three passes around the field, leaving a bare ring around the still un-mowed center. I parked in the field and sat on the hood of my rental car. When Uncle Pete pulled up even with me and stopped, I climbed up beside him on the tractor and leaned against the fender. We drove twice around the field without talking before I asked him: "You figure out who I am yet?"

"Well," he said, "I know you're one of John's boys. I ain't figured out which one yet."

Making hay is a fairly involved process. The hay must be at the right growth stage so that the plants are full of nutrients. The weather must cooperate so that you can mow the hay, rake it into windrows (long piles) that dry in the sun, then turn the windrows so that the hay on the bottom of the pile dries. If the hay does not dry properly it can later rot in the barn. If the hay is really wet the heat given off while it rots can set the entire barn on fire.

After the sun and breeze remove just the right amount of water from the hay, the baling machine then scoops up the windrow, packs the hay into rectangular bales, and ties the bales with twine. The baling machine spits the bale out the back onto a wagon where someone stacks the bales for transport back to the barn. Each bale weighs about 60 pounds, and they are stacked six or seven high on the wagon.

When the wagon is full, someone - usually an older child - drives up in a tractor pulling an empty wagon. You stop, switch wagons, and the full wagon is pulled to the barn for unloading while the empty wagon is hitched to the baler and filled.

Back at the barn, the wagons are unloaded onto an elevator, which is just like an escalator for hay bales. The elevator carries the bales up into the barn's hayloft, where two or three people tightly stack the bales for storage until the hay is later fed to the livestock.

On some larger farms, some of these jobs are automated or eliminated using different techniques, but on my cousin's farm you need at least six or seven people to make the process work smoothly.

I rode around the field with my uncle a few more times, then got my car and drove up to the house to see where they wanted my help. My cousin was gone for the morning playing at a basketball tournament, but his dad and brother were out gathering wagons and mowing another field. I visited with my cousin's wife and his five daughters for a while before they came back

By mid-afternoon that farm was incredibly busy. We baled hay with two crews from four fields. They showed me how to stack hay while bouncing around the field on a slippery wooden wagon. Men and women from all over the county had shown up, and at one time there were 18 people helping in one way or another. One of my cousin's teen-age daughters came up on the wagon to help me stack hay and was throwing the bales one-handed to the top of the stack over six feet in the air. I spent some time driving the tractors running wagons from the barn to the fields and back. I even tried to work in the hayloft, but the incredible dust and heat quickly drove me out. "Drink more beer," my cousins assured me. "You'll be all right soon."

At Sunday dinner the next day, surrounded by family I hadn't seen for years, eating and laughing and talking, I asked my cousin how he'd scheduled all the help. Surely all these people were busy and had their own lives to live. How did he get them all to come over and work such dirty jobs, especially when he couldn't know in advance when the weather would be good for making hay?

He didn't really understand the question. "Well," he said, "they saw us mowing."

I got in my car that evening and drove back to Detroit. By the time I reached the motel I knew that my life had to change. I was working long hours for good money but spent a lot of time solving problems that didn't mean anything. I really liked building machines that made cars better and the lives of the car builders easier, but I wasn't interested in the infantile bickering and game-playing of corporate life. I decided that it was important to include my children in my work and my life, and to become more involved in their lives.

Mermaid on the hard for hurricane season.

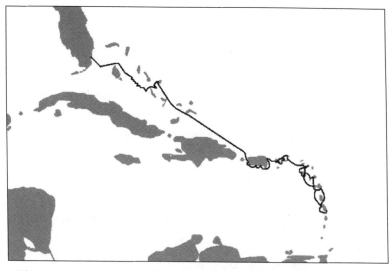

The trip route, starting in St. Maarten in the Northeast Corner of the Caribbean Islands, and ending in Ft. Lauterdale.

What Were We Thinking?

What eventually became a great ocean-going sailing voyage
originally had nothing to do with sailing. My wife, Nancy, and I
wanted to home-school our kids for a year, and we wanted a family
adventure. Our third-grade son, Pender, and our sixth-grade
daughter, Lena, both had good friends and did well in school, but
we wanted to spend more time with them before setting them loose
in the trials and potential peril of adolescence. We hoped that the
lessons learned in a great adventure would help to protect them
during what we remembered as the horror of middle school, and we
believed that real character that protects us during adversity is
created and maintained only by facing and overcoming real challenges. It was important to us that we pursue something new to all
of us that would be difficult to complete. We wanted a trip that
would present problems and challenges that we could solve only as
a family.

Nancy and I are both mechanical engineers, and we were looking
forward to personally teaching our kids. We hoped to give them a
more fundamental base for future learning, with more emphasis on
math, reading and writing than they were getting at school.

All four of us were active boaters in Puget Sound in Washington
and the Gulf Islands in British Columbia, and we often spent week-
ends and longer on our 24-foot power boat.

We discussed buying a motor home and spending a year seeing
North America, but staying in crowded campgrounds and
driving a great big shoebox just wasn't attractive to us. We
discussed getting a larger powerboat and traveling from Seattle
to Alaska and back, but cold, wet weather didn't seem like a
good feature for a family adventure.

Nancy and I had spent our 10th wedding anniversary at a resort
on Raratonga in the Cook Islands in the South Pacific. We
loved it there, and naively considered buying a sailboat and

cruising the great round trip from Seattle to San Diego to Baja Mexico to Tahiti to the South Pacific to Hawaii, and back to Seattle. A little research showed that this is a two-year or longer trip and the long passages would be very dull or uncomfortable for Lena and Pender.

We liked the idea of a sailing trip, though, so we did more research on two options: the Sea of Cortez in Mexico and the Caribbean. We'd been to Baja a few times and really liked the area, the friendly people, the beautiful water and the great fishing. But we knew that facilities in Mexico were often primitive and that the Caribbean had several charter fleets based throughout the islands. We knew that the Caribbean charter fleets would support a larger service base, hopefully making repairs and parts easier to get. The Caribbean it was.

Before this trip, Nancy, Lena and Pender had spent very little time on sailboats. I had done some dinghy sailing and club racing with friends, and Nancy and I had been crew on two one-week sailing charters in the BVI (British Virgin Islands). She and I had taken both the Coast Guard and U.S. Power Squadron boating safety classes, and we were both good at pilotage (local navigation) and anchoring. I am a reasonably good mechanic, and Lena and Pender know how to behave on boats and handle dinghies. We didn't know much about sailboat cruising or what to look for when buying a sailboat. We were extremely lucky, in fact incredibly extremely lucky, to get some of the best advice imaginable.

Before we sold the Fisheye underwater video camera product line we had developed, two of our cameras were installed on a 150-foot megayacht built to support the America's Cup effort in New Zealand. The project manager for that boat was David Darwent. David knows almost everything about yacht construction and operation and was also a Caribbean charter captain for some time. He was happy to help us with our project, and he also introduced us to his friend Bruce Schattenburg, a broker from Fort Lauderdale. As it turns out,

Bruce is one of the premier brokers in the country, concentrating mostly on very large yachts. He and his wife, Jennifer Saia, run The Sacks Group Yachting Professionals. The more I learn about both of these men the more amazed and grateful I am that they took the time to help us prepare for our trip.

Our original plan was to buy a boat in the United States and start our trip in Southern Florida. We felt that moving onto the boat would be a big enough first step, and that outfitting and provisioning it would be much easier in the United States than, say, the BVI. Nancy and I found a suitable boat on the Internet and, working through Bruce, negotiated a purchase price dependent on survey and buyer inspection. I flew to Fort Lauderdale to inspect the ex-charter boat, which had just been sailed to Ft. Lauderdale. The boat was in good shape and the sails and diesel engine were in good to fair condition. However, there was some fiberglass damage on the transom and rust spots on the iron keel that required repair. We presented a counter-offer to the seller, decreasing the purchase price to cover the repairs. While waiting for the seller's reply I spent some more time on the boat inspecting, inventorying, and measuring so that we could start shopping for and making the things we would need for our trip. Some letters and receipts I found on the boat showed that the engine might have recently seized and been rebuilt. We immediately requested clarification from the seller. When they didn't answer we withdrew our offer.

Bruce quickly found a great boat in St. Maarten, a small island on the northeast "corner" of the Caribbean chain. It is one-half Dutch (Sint Maarten) and one-half French (Saint Martin). Bruce was ready to fly to St. Maarten the next day and inspect the boat but I didn't have my passport with me in Florida. I was also not convinced that a tiny island in the middle of nowhere was the best place to buy a boat. I was wrong. Starting in St. Maarten was the best thing we could have done.

Bruce and Dave took me to dinner and explained to me, in highly technical terms: "It's windy in the Caribbean, and the wind blows from the east." Therefore, starting a Caribbean trip in Florida means that you spend the first part of the trip going straight upwind for over a thousand miles. Many cruisers never make it past the Bahamas. They spend the entire winter in Georgetown waiting for the trade winds to stop blowing. For our family, with little sailing experience and no open-ocean experience, the trip into the wind would have been a disaster. Dave gave me a copy of "The Gentleman's Guide to Passages South," by Bruce Van Sant. This 250-page book is written specifically to help people make this series of passages, called the "Thorny Path", from Florida to the Virgin Islands and south. We used this book and its straightforward advice throughout the trip, but its main value was helping us decide to start the trip down-island.

A few weeks later in May, Bruce and I flew to St. Maarten, inspected and sailed *Cibonet*, and had her stored on land for Hurricane season. (Cibonet, pronounced see-bow-neigh, is the French spelling for one of the groups of people that lived in the Caribbean before European exploration and conquest. There are no Cibonet people left.)

We spent the rest of the spring, summer, and early fall at our home on Camano Island, Washington, getting ready for the trip. We read every guide and cruising book we could find, Nancy took sailing lessons and crewed during some club races, the kids took swimming lessons and a correspondence boating course from the U.S. Power Squadron, and we made lists and lists of things to buy and pack. St. Maarten is a duty - free port, so you can import anything you want without customs or duty hassles, and half of the island is a French province, so you can get yachting equipment from France at a deep discount. For instance, we ordered a Zodiac life raft for pickup in St. Maarten for about two-thirds its U.S. cost. Other marine supplies are available in St. Maarten from two large marine chain stores. Prices are about the same as U.S. retail prices, although the selection is slightly less. General supplies and provisions are also easy to get there, with several large retail and food stores on the island.

We arranged for a friend of a friend to stay in our house while we were gone. She paid a small rent equal to the property taxes and other fixed costs, and paid for all her utility charges. She took great care of the house, and it was reassuring for us that the house wasn't empty while we were gone.

On September 11, 2001, about one and a half months before our departure date, a small group of hateful men destroyed the lives of thousands of people in New York City. Although the future of the country and our economy looked uncertain, we kept to our plans. Staying home and missing the trip seemed like a bigger risk.

Bananas in St. Maarten.

From: Phil, Nancy, Lena and Pender
To: Mermaid Distribution
Email Sent: October 19, 2001

Notice: This is your best chance to remove your name from this list and prevent receiving any future mailings about the Rinks' boat trip. Just email us back to this address and ask us to remove your name. No hard feelings. Also email us if you want us to use a different address, or add someone else.

Hello, everyone:

We leave home one week from tomorrow. We will spend three days in Ft. Lauderdale at the boat show, then on to St. Maarten and onto the boat, and are 90 percent packed, with only 50 percent of the packing left to do. We are trying very hard to fit everything into our allotment of two bags plus one carry-on plus one purse or laptop per person. It looks like we're taking about 700 pounds of stuff total. I have no idea what it all is. About 20 pounds of it is clothes.

We've met with the kids' teachers and have all their school materials packed. No sweat so far.

Lena is done with her club soccer games for the season. She will miss the last game of the season next Saturday afternoon. She will ref three games tomorrow, then will be done reffing. She also has one or two school games next week.

Pender has his last soccer game tomorrow. He will also miss a game next Saturday.

Lena will take both a flute and a saxophone. I am really looking forward to anchoring next to a chartered megayacht so that Lena can have an audience for her sax practice.

Lena has been training a dog to become an assistance dog for kids in wheelchairs. She has done a great job. That dog, Abby, goes on to advanced training next Tuesday. We anticipate that even if Abby washes out of training, they will use her for breeding because she really is an amazing puppy.

This is our anticipated schedule, for those of you who wish to meet up with us at some point:

Arrive St. Maarten: October 30.
Head south, possibly as far as Grenada: mid to late December.
Arrive back in St. Maarten: late February
Head west (BVI/PR/Bahamas): mid March
Arrive Houston to load the boat on a trailer and ship to Seattle: June.

This is our real schedule:

Arrive St. Maarten: October 30.

If you do want to meet up with us, let us know what dates you want to come and we'll try to keep you updated with our plans for that date. Remember to stay flexible with your arrangements to accommodate our last - minute changes in plans due to weather. You also might want to make sure your passport is good and start working on a tan.

We will not be exchanging gifts with anyone this holiday season. Please don't try to send us anything. It seems like it's really a nightmare. Thanks anyway.

Thanks to everyone for your support. For those of you that are worried about us traveling now, I can't imagine anywhere in the world currently safer than the Caribbean, except maybe Camano Island, WA. I hope you are all safe.

Phil, Nancy, Lena and Pender Rink

"Those that give up essential liberty to obtain a little temporary safety deserve neither liberty nor safety, and will in the end have neither." - Benjamin Franklin, 1784

Buying and Equipping the Boat

We had a pretty good idea what type of boat we wanted. The Beneteau Oceanis 400 is a real workhorse of the Caribbean charter industry. Its three-cabin/two-head layout, with symmetrical aft cabins for the kids and a forward cabin with its own head for Mom and Dad fit our needs exactly. The sloop rig sail plan is simple and robust. A sloop rig means that there is one mast and two triangular sails, the headsail (also called the jib or Genoa) forward and the mainsail aft. The headsail stores rolled onto the forestay and the mainsail stores on its own roller inside the mast. All the sail control lines lead to the cockpit, and four easily reached winches make line control simple. Any of us, including nine-year-old Pender, could reef (make the sail smaller) or stow the sails quickly.

People make two major criticisms of Beneteau sailboats. First, they consider it a lightly built production boat. Well, it is a light production boat. In fact, it's light because it's a production boat. Parts fit together well and interlock to provide extra strength. The Beneteaus are very well suited to Caribbean and coastal sailing. The second common criticism is that Beneteaus are not meant for passage making. There certainly have been lots of Beneteaus that have crossed oceans and made long passages. If we wanted to cross an ocean, we would spend some time improving the battery mounts and fastening the floor panels. However, cruising the Caribbean is not open ocean travel. A typical passage is 40 to 70 nautical miles and takes about 10 hours, anchor up to anchor down. You can wait in sheltered harbors for weather, and most of your time on the boat is spent anchored.

Roller furling sails were crucial to the success of our trip. Roller furling headsails are common, and only sailing purists and racers use "hanked-on" headsails that must be dropped to the deck and stowed. The mast - stowed roller furling mainsail is less common and slightly more problematic. Because it must roll easily into the mast, our mainsail was made lighter than many cruising mainsails. It cannot use battens (stiffening boards of wood or fiberglass placed in pockets in the sail) to stiffen the roach (free side) of the sail, and the roach must be concave rather than convex, decreasing the area and therefore the drive of the sail. Racers or performance-minded sailors will never have in-mast roller furling on their boat.

However, for a family of four with little sailing experience the in-mast furling mainsail was perfect. We ordered a brand new mainsail for our trip, opting for a Neil Pride sail made to Beneteau specifications rather than a higher-end "custom" sail, and had the sail delivered directly to St. Maarten to avoid duty and shipping charges. The sail fit the mast exactly and performed well. It stowed and deployed easily. We never had a jam, even when we stowed or reefed the sail while sailing downwind. The boat's lack of performance sailing to weather meant nothing to us because we preferred to start the engine and motor-sail, keeping just enough wind in the severely reefed mainsail to steady the boat but not enough to lean the boat over.

One of the most important features on the Oceanis 400, both for safety and convenience, is the open "sugar scoop" transom. It made it easy for us to get in and out of the boat. It was great for loading supplies and groceries from the dinghy. If you fall overboard from a classic ocean cruiser with its high smooth sides and transom you might not be able to climb back aboard, even at anchor in a calm harbor. With the open transom it was easy to climb aboard, with or without the boarding ladder.

The boat we chose and named *Mermaid* had been originally purchased for a charter company but was promptly beached by Hurricane Luis in 1995. Luis was a category 4 hurricane with 140-knot winds that destroyed more than a thousand boats in St. Maarten. Purchased out of salvage after Luis, our future boat was repaired and returned to the sea with only some slight stress cracks in the deck gelcoat and some scratches in the woodwork. There was no staining or wire corrosion, so it was apparent that the hull had not sunk.

Mermaid had originally been registered in St. Maarten. We hired an agent in Florida through our broker to document the vessel with the U.S. Coast Guard in order to insure clear title. Documentation is also required to cruise the French islands in the Caribbean. The boat has never had state registration in the United States, and state registration is not required anywhere in the Caribbean.

Any Caribbean ex-charter boat will be sufficiently equipped to support a one-year cruise through the islands, and will be better equipped than many of the full-time cruising boats in the area. We made a number of additions to Mermaid, mostly to increase our margin of safety, but also for our comfort.

Our plan was to sell the boat when we got home. In fact, because the same boat sold for about $30,000 more in Seattle, we hoped that the boat would pay for the trip. We tried not to add fixed equipment that would not increase her sales price once we returned home. Her basic mechanical features were great, and the owner had recently added an autopilot and wind generator. We added a new mainsail, a watermaker, and a GPS (Global Positioning System) with integral mapping software. We didn't get a full-featured chart plotter because we planned on using paper charts and guidebooks when close to land. We also added a backup storm anchor (a Fortress) with 200 feet of 5/8" nylon rode, and a life raft.

We knew that we would be using lots of electricity with two laptop computers, digital video and still cameras, radios, and reading lights. We also knew that the two existing group 27 house batteries would not provide adequate power for long-term use. However, we hoped the wind generator would help keep the batteries charged, and we knew that we could always simply run the motor and charge the batteries if required. Once we were underway, I wished that I had installed a large capacity alternator with an external controller. Using a bigger alternator would probably have cut the battery charge time in half, because the stock alternator was only designed to restore the charge on the starting battery. It would quit charging at high current well before the house battery bank was fully charged.

The wind generator proved to be just about as annoying as it was helpful. It was extremely loud and the stress caused by that noise (usually on a rough passage or in a stormy anchorage) was often not worth the small amount of power generated. There were a few times, such as when we anchored in Nonsuch Bay on Antigua, where the anchorage was not sheltered, and the constant 18-25 knot winds generated enough electricity to keep the batteries full for three or four days. Most anchorages were more sheltered, and 5-10 knot winds were not strong enough to drive the generator and create useful power.

The previous owner of our boat had installed small, dedicated reading lights in each cabin to reduce power consumption. If we were going to live on and own the boat for some time, I would install power-saving LED light bulbs in these fixtures. For our one-year trip it was much cheaper to simply run the engine a little more often. In general we did spend a lot of time and energy trying to conserve battery power. Leaving one small reading light on for the day, or falling asleep with the light on, would use a considerable amount of power.

We used an inexpensive portable 1,000-watt inverter to convert the 12-volt DC battery power to 120-volt AC power for the computers and the battery chargers. During the trip, the batteries on both laptop computers failed. It is not clear whether they were damaged somehow by inverter/charger interaction. We could have, and probably should have, bought "car adapters" for the computers to power them directly off the 12-volt boat batteries.

Our watermaker was a Village Marine "Little Wonder." It uses a titanium piston pump driven by a 12-volt motor to pressurize highly filtered seawater to 800 PSI. High pressure is needed to force fresh water through the watermaker's reverse-osmosis membrane, creating a trickle of fresh water that we would run into our storage tanks and an extra-salty waste stream that is pumped back overboard. We were glad to have our own fresh water source, as good fresh water can be difficult to find and expensive in the Caribbean. Other boats had watermakers, bought water, and/or captured rainwater by diverting the deck drains into the water tanks. Many boats were able to capture enough rainwater that they never had to buy water. One boat we met installed a diverter valve to bottle pure water right out of the watermaker for drinking. They used tank water for washing and cooking. That would have been a good modification to our system.

Our engine-driven cold plate worked great to keep our food cold, but it was also the biggest maintenance problem on the boat. We had it serviced in three ports and two languages before I got out the reference books and figured out we needed a new filter/dryer. After that it worked really well until the clutch on the compressor gave out in the Bahamas. It was late in the trip, and parts are difficult to get in the Bahamas, so we gave up and bought ice for the last three weeks of the trip. When the cold plate system worked it worked really well. The refrigeration was almost free since we had to run the motor for at least an hour a day to charge the batteries. Actually, maybe the electricity was almost free since we had to run the motor to keep our food cold.

Of all the dangers we faced on our trip, the thing I feared most was lightning. We installed a small lightning dissipater at the top of the mast. A lightning dissipater has lots of sharp pointed wires. Each point bleeds any electrical charge on the boat or the rigging harmlessly into the air, keeping them from building up to a charge big enough to attract lightning. Ours was made from an unraveled piece of stainless wire rope and was simply screwed into the masthead with self-tapping stainless steel screws. We made sure that the mast was electrically well bonded to the iron keel, and hoped for the best.

The boat came with a diaphragm-style bilge pump, which was perfectly adequate for pumping out condensation or the small amount of rainwater that would find its way into the boat. It was not large enough or clog-proof enough to keep the boat from sinking in the event of even a small leak. We brought a large, 1,750 gallon-per-hour electric auxiliary bilge pump, which we could plug into the cigarette lighter socket in an emergency. An attached 10-foot hose would direct the water into the self-draining cockpit. We never used it.

Since we were starting at the upwind end of the islands our 40-gallon fuel tank was large enough. Had we started in Florida we would have installed more fuel capacity, possibly using jerry cans or a flexible bladder tank. We did have one five-gallon jerry can we used to carry fuel from shore. We had to use it once, in the Bahamas.

We brought about 20 pounds of tools with us on the airplane, and there was already a fair tool kit on the boat. We also bought some tools in St. Maarten and elsewhere along the way. We didn't have every tool we needed, but we had enough to make do. There are many places in the Caribbean where you can get your boat repaired, but our boat usually wasn't broken when we were in those places.

It's not easy to find a good place to install a TV/VCR in a Beneteau, but the previous owners had done a really nice job. We immediately removed the TV and the nice swing mount and sold them on the morning cruiser radio net in St. Maarten. Other than the laptop computers, we didn't have any computer games on board.

We bought hull insurance from a broker in St. Maarten. At the time, we were told that the underwriter was from Lloyds of London, and we thought all was well. Toward the end of our trip, we found out that the underwriter was actually from Poland, and our broker disappeared in the middle of a fraud scandal. We still don't know whether we had any insurance during the trip. From what we heard, the Seven Seas Cruising Association (SSCA) might be the best source for insurance.

There were lots of small, slow dinghies in the Caribbean, some powered with two-horsepower outboards. Our boat came with a 10 ½-foot inflatable RIB (rigid inflatable boat) and a 15-HP Mercury outboard motor. A RIB has a fiberglass (sometimes aluminum) hull surrounded by an inflatable tubular ring. The sturdy hull can carry a larger outboard motor and provide a good planing surface for speed, while the tubular sides make good seats and are gentle to the boats you bump into. Although our dinghy was heavy-280 pounds without the motor-and hard to get onto the foredeck for passages, we were glad for her speed and carrying capacity. A smaller, less powerful dinghy would have soaked us in one- or two-foot chop. She did have a persistent leak in the bottom, and despite our diligent patching efforts we usually started dinghy trips by removing the drain plug while underway so that the water could run out from inside the hollow fiberglass floor. We towed the dinghy while sailing in calm water, and lifted it onto the foredeck for inter-island passages. The outboard motor was stored on a bracket on the stern rail. The six-gallon gas tank was more than adequate, and we didn't carry any extra gasoline.

We spent some time coming up with a name and logo for our boat. We really wanted to involve the kids in the project, so we didn't want a name that was too esoteric or obscure. We also wanted to avoid problematic names. For instance: There is a beautiful old schooner out of Victoria, British Columbia, named *Passing Cloud*. Locally, everyone knows her as *Passing Wind*.

We had iron-on transfers made of the *Mermaid* logo in three sizes, and then made crew shirts, hats, and sweat pants out of regular clothing. Your boat name is especially important while cruising, because it becomes your name. Your boat name is your radio call sign, your account name at the marine store, your bar tab, and your social name (I was Phil from *Mermaid*). If you or your crew likes to spend a lot of time yakking on the radio, your boat name will become an annoyance and a joke to the rest of the cruising community. We had a local vinyl sign company make our transom decoration and we applied it when we got to St. Maarten. We could have had the transfer made there.

St. Maarten was indeed the best place we could have begun our trip. The Dutch side speaks English, primarily, and Dutch, officially. The French side speaks French, primarily, and enough English to get by. There are surveyors, mechanics, parts, riggers, sail-makers, and refrigeration mechanics, mostly located right on the lagoon so you can get to them by dinghy. There is easily accessible food, clothing, and general shopping. Best of all, the cruising community is solid and open, with a well-attended cruising net every morning on VHF channel 14 at 7:30 run by Jack from *Davina*. Jack is a local cruiser and business owner. The St. Maarten Yacht Club is a great place to meet people and get experienced cruising and sailing advice, as well as a cold drink and a hot meal.

Nancy and Pender.

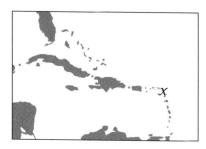

From: Phil, Nancy, Lena and Pender
To: Mermaid Distribution
Email Sent: November 8, 2001

It's Sunday night. We have the boat anchored in the middle of the bay for the second night, tonight. Last night was my first good night's sleep on the island, but Nancy, for the first time, didn't sleep well. Pender, remarkably, slept in the cockpit. He says he is going to sleep in the cockpit for the rest of the trip. We'll see when it starts raining.

Lena is playing her flute, and Pender is playing along on the harmonica. It actually sounds pretty good.

The boat is in great shape. We have had to do very little in terms of "fixing" her. We have been very busy trying to get our new equipment installed while we still have a rental car (we turn it in on Wednesday). The watermaker is almost completely installed, and hopefully we'll get the mast stepped (stood upright) on Tuesday. We're having a professional company do it so they'll check everything as it goes up. Right now the mast is sitting on the deck, in the way of everything. The sails are packed into the kids' cabins.

Today for a break we loaded into the dinghy (a 10'6" hard bottom inflatable with a 15-HP outboard) and went out into the ocean. We found a little reef and went snorkeling. Even though the bottom was mostly sandy, and the water was a little turbid, we had a great time. Pender was a snorkeling monster. He didn't want to get out of the water.

We have been eating all of our meals at the local Yacht Club (which is four shipping containers arranged in two parallel lines of two containers with a tarp roof). Very tasty, extremely tropical, and very friendly. Tonight, though, Nancy and the kids went shopping and we had a cooked meal on the boat. Pork and rice. Very nice.

Mosquitoes ate Pender the first night. We were sleeping on the boat, with the boat on the shore. Out here on the bay, though, there are no bugs and we leave the windows and hatches open all night.

Since we don't have a mast, we don't have a radio antenna, and we don't get any weather reports. However, we understand that there is a huge hurricane over Cuba right now. Nobody here is concerned, and we wish the Floridians getting this good luck. We're trying to keep track in case it turns east like Lenny did last year. So far, so good.

We did have a small problem getting out of Florida on the way down. Despite a daily call to Florida Shuttle express, they sent a regular cab to pick up us and our 17 pieces of luggage. By the time they found a larger taxi, we ended up at the airport only 57 minutes before our flight. FAA requires 60 minutes, to insure our luggage goes on our flight. So, we spent an extra day in Miami. The helpful ticket agent for American Airlines found us an inexpensive room nearby. If anyone needs a threadbare room with fleas directly under the Miami runway, we know the place for you.

We didn't have the same problem leaving Seattle because a friend of ours, Jack Gunter (yes, that Jack Gunter) got up very early and drove us to the airport one week ago yesterday. Thanks, Jack.

Lena says it's hot.

Pender says we're working too hard so far. He's sure it will get better.

The kids have had two days of school so far. They did their schoolwork at the yacht club, with the trade wind blowing through their hair. Not such a bad life.

Lena also says it's windy, the water is cold, and it's about like Stanwood. Lena is more of a teenager than we thought. Bummer.

We are anchored right under the end of the runway, so about 10 times a day big jets (including two 747s per day) take off directly overhead.

That's all for now. We hope you are all well.

Love,
Phil, Nancy, Lena and Pender

It's now Thursday noon. I'm off to the gendarmes to see if we are legally in the country or not. I hope we are. Obviously email is more of a problem than we thought it would be. I'll try to get it sorted out today.

Thanks to Mom and Stan who sent us Iridium messages. I wish there was a quick way to acknowledge "message received." It sounds like Lena's soccer team finished the season with a bang. Great job, girls. We bought a soccer ball at the local Costco (called "Buy4Less").

The mast and rigging is all up and in. The remnants of the outskirts of the tropical wave associated with Hurricane Michelle are blowing through today, so it's windy and occasionally rainy. Pender and Lena were sleeping outside last night when they got hammered by a squall. Wet pillows are OK, right? They'll dry, right? When it stops blowing we'll install the sails.

The kids had school on the boat today for the first time. That is quite an accomplishment, because it means we got enough stuff stowed that we could use the cabin table.

That's all for now. Pender and I are going to dinghy to shore in the gale. Wish us well.

We don't get much news. Hope the country is well.

Phil, Nancy, Lena and Pender

School

One of the main reasons for taking a family trip was to have an excuse to pull our kids out of school for a year and try to "reset" their behavior where we saw problems developing. Both Lena and Pender were good students, but their writing and spelling abilities were not being challenged, and they were being taught math and science using curriculum that used bizarre terms like "number sentence" instead of "equation."

Nancy and I knew we could teach math and science, and were not too concerned about teaching writing and spelling since the support materials for those subjects were good. For geography and history we figured we could do as well as the schools. Physical education could take care of itself.

We met with the kids' teachers in October. Where possible, we bought or borrowed the books used and the lesson plans for those books. Some teachers actually let us borrow books to finish the year, and we found the others in used-book stores and on the Internet. We also brought our own reference materials.

On board we made school top priority when we were anchored. The kids worked to lesson plans that Nancy wrote out weekly, and for the most part worked on their own. There was some give-and-take when the kids wanted more or less supervision or support, but we usually let them work on their own and ask for help when they needed it. We did school seven days a week when we could. This left us free to take several days off in a row to explore special places like Les Saintes in Guadeloupe or Anegada in the British Virgin Islands.

For math, Pender was learning fractions and long division, and Lena was learning algebra. Neatness and penmanship is crucial for both of these skills, and both were fairly sloppy writers. We spent extra time emphasizing neatness and handwriting, and they both really improved.

Sometimes letting the kids set their own pace backfired. There were a few times that Lena would work a week or two ahead missing one of the key issues of the lesson (and getting all the problems wrong). Nobody had any fun while she re-did the work.

Every week or two, the kids would have to write a five-paragraph essay. These essays use a fixed format and were a staple of my education. Apparently they have fallen out of favor, but the ability to get ideas down on paper clearly and quickly only becomes more important as the kids get older. The essay format never changes. In paragraph one you summarize what you are going to say and in paragraph five you summarize what you said and draw conclusions. Paragraphs two through four present three main ideas, each with three or more sub-topics. The first essays took two or three days to write, but by the end of the trip both Pender and Lena could knock out a cogent essay in about three hours. Now the essays have become an important tool for us to resolve conflict and communicate with each other (for example: "Write an essay on why you want to go skiing this weekend and then we'll talk about it").

We brought a 70-pound Rubbermaid tub of books with us to the Caribbean. Most were children's paperback books. The kids were done reading these by December. There are very few bookstores in the Caribbean, and almost none that carry children's books. Luckily, we met up with some other family cruisers in January and were able to trade with them for other books. By the end of the trip, Lena and Pender were both reading adult books for pleasure, such as Steven Ambrose's "Undaunted Courage" and the Hobbit trilogy.

The biggest barrier to successful schooling on the boat was the lack of positive and negative rewards that we could use as teacher/parents to motivate the kids. There was no competition within a peer group. They knew that we would go see the local fort in the afternoon whether their schoolwork was done or not.

They knew that if they got perfect grades on the next test there wouldn't be any special rewards, because there weren't any to give. We did every special thing we could find anyway. Eventually, we fell to setting a minimum standard (85% on a math test, for instance), that they had to meet before proceeding. Nobody liked that solution. For the most part, though, the kids did their own work and did it fairly well. Now that we are back home, the kids improved work habits and self-reliance really help them at school.

The formal part of school would last for about two to three hours a day. There is no question that their education was at least as good as they would have received at home in their regular schools. In addition, of course, they learned a lot about themselves and the world that they would not have learned in school. For instance, they both became much more trusting of their own judgment and much less susceptible to peer pressure.

That being said, both kids (and both parents) were more than ready to return to public schools. The kids missed their friends and activities of school, and all of us welcomed the reduction in conflict that comes from separating scholastic and family life. They did have to "re-enter" school and re-establish their social standing and friendships. However, they did this with increased self-image and reliance on their own capabilities and strengths, with less emphasis on peer pressure and dependence on others.

Lena brought both her saxophone and her flute. She practiced enough on both to stay competent, but without a band to play with it was difficult for her to stay motivated. I had hoped to buy a used guitar in a pawn shop so we could play together but was surprised to find that there aren't any pawn shops in the Caribbean, and the cheapest guitar I could find was about $300 for a very poorly made instrument.

Both kids were encouraged to write in their journals, but the journals were entirely for their use. We never read them.

Most other family boats that we met used the Calvert School program. This is a correspondence school that is set up to review work and administer tests by email. We don't know the quality of the education, but the program would certainly reduce family stress and encourage student performance because a non-parent assigns and grades the students' work.

School.

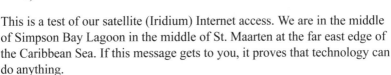

From: Phil, Nancy, Lena and Pender
To: Mermaid Distribution
Email Sent: November 12, 2001

Hello, all:

This is a test of our satellite (Iridium) Internet access. We are in the middle of Simpson Bay Lagoon in the middle of St. Maarten at the far east edge of the Caribbean Sea. If this message gets to you, it proves that technology can do anything.

First of all, we heard briefly about the tragedy in NY today. [Note: an airliner flying from New York City to the Dominican Republic had crashed soon after takeoff. It was not apparent whether further terrorism was involved. It later turned out that it was a "normal" crash.] It sometimes seems that we should be home at times like this, but what would we be doing that would matter? Maybe it is a rationalization (my major in college), but doing what we normally do seems like the best part for most of us to play.

Today we sailed east to Philipsburg and touristed around, where we saw the news in an electronics shop, then sailed back to our present home here in Simpson Bay Lagoon. Pender and Lena got a short bit of snorkeling in the first clear water we've seen (the lagoon and bay are cloudy from surf and dredging) and we did our first "open water" sailing in four to five foot seas and 15-knot winds.

The watermaker and GPS work great. Tomorrow we buy and install new batteries. Space considerations mean that we won't have enough batteries to keep them from discharging too much. If we were keeping the boat longer, we would do major surgery and add more batteries. As it is, batteries are cheaper than boat modifications.

We're almost done "fixing" the boat. We've taken two day sails (counting today), and will day sail for about two more weeks before attempting our first "voyage." Baby steps. Baby steps.

That's all for now. Keep safe.

Phil, Nancy, Lena and Pender Rink

Anchoring

At home in Puget Sound we rarely spend a night on the boat anchored. The sea bottom there is either steep rocky slopes or muddy flats fouled with card-table-size kelp fronds. In the islands, we spent every night but three at anchor or on a mooring buoy. The tropical bottom was almost always clean sand, 15 to 25 feet deep. Mermaid had a huge plough anchor (about 35 pounds) and 30 meters (100 feet) of 10mm (3/8-inch) chain, with another 30 meters of ¾ inch nylon rode. Although many boats had all-chain rode, the mixed chain/rope was perfectly satisfactory. We rarely used much of the rope portion of the rode, and it almost never reached the bottom where it could potentially chafe on coral. The plough anchor was very easy to set, and it held well. We never anchored in mud, but if we had we would have used our Fortress fluke-type anchor.

We took our time anchoring, often re-setting once or twice to get it just right. Nancy would work the bow and have complete control. Using hand signals, she would guide the boat into the right position, ask me for the depth, and then lower the anchor to the bottom using the electric windlass. Once the anchor was on the bottom, I would back the boat downwind while Nancy paid out more chain. We would generally use about a 5:1 scope, depending on how crowded the anchorage was. In other words, we would use all 100 feet of anchor chain when anchoring in water 20 feet deep. We would back down gradually until the chain came tight, then increase to full throttle to set the anchor. Nancy would feel the chain to see if we were dragging. If the anchor slipped through the sandy bottom or skated over a hard coral bottom the chain would vibrate. Often the water was clear and calm enough that she could see the anchor as it hit the bottom. Later, one or both of us almost always snorkeled on the anchor to make sure it set correctly.

We used a second anchor if there was shallow water within the swing area or if we were on a lee shore.

In the Virgin Islands and Puerto Rico mooring buoys were common and often mandatory. There was much more life on the bottom in areas where buoy use was required, as anchor and rode damage in popular anchorages kept the sand scoured clean. Some moorings, especially in the USVI and Puerto Rico, were free. The buoys in the BVI were private and cost $20 per night which added up quickly. Most of the anchorages in the BVI are either very deep or very crowded and it's difficult to avoid using a mooring.

Our biggest anchoring worry was other boats. Right before Christmas, in crowded Falmouth Harbor in Antigua, we anchored between a beautiful large wooden schooner and a cliff. We thought we had plenty of clearance to both. Soon after dark a bizarre storm blew through the harbor. It brought 50-knot winds straight out of the north, swinging us 90 degrees and trying to blow us onto the rocks. We had seven feet of water under our six-foot keel and about 20 feet between our stern and the rocks behind us. Worse than that, the unattended schooner had swung within three feet of us. We later found that he had 200 feet of chain out in 25 feet of water. We started the motor and spent the next several hours powering into the wind and away from the schooner. We didn't dare raise the anchor because it was very difficult to hold the bow into the wind. If we went sideways to the wind between the time when the anchor was holding us in place and the anchor was on deck we could easily have ended up on the rocks or into our neighbor. There were also lots of unlit boats in the harbor, and it was unclear what we would have done once we recovered the anchor. The same storm brought 60 knots of wind to Nonsuch Bay on the east side of the island and several boats sank or were beached. We moved the next morning to the eastern (upwind) end of the harbor, and from then on always tried to anchor in the "front row" in crowded anchorages.

After that experience we tired of other boats anchoring close upwind. We also noticed that it was difficult to tell where other boats' anchors were when we tried to pick our anchoring spot. We bought an eight-inch pink buoy in Pointe a Pitre, Guadeloupe, and used it as our anchor buoy. We tied a 30-foot line to the head of our anchor, ran it through the eye of our new buoy, and then tied the free end to a two-pound weight. The weight would pull the slack line through the buoy eye so that the buoy would float directly over our anchor. Instantly, other boats gave us more anchoring room. The buoy also made it easier to raise anchor, because I could drive the bow of the boat directly over the anchor while Nancy winched in the chain. Our anchor buoy was a real help during the trip, and we continued to use it even in the Bahamas, where anchor buoys are strangely illegal.

For most of the trip we lost a lot of sleep worrying about dragging anchor during the night. Later in the trip we decided that we knew more about anchoring and did a better job than most cruisers, and very few of them ended up on the beach. On our next trip we will use the same anchoring techniques, but we will have more confidence in our abilities and worry less.

From: Phil, Nancy, Lena and Pender
To: Mermaid Distribution
Email Sent: November 22, 2001

Hello to all from St. Maarten! We are back in Simpson Bay from Anguilla, to make the final repairs/improvements to the boat and then head south. We want to send more pictures, but are having difficulties figuring out how to get the email list onto a disk so we can use a shore line to send the larger files.

We hope you all have (or are having) a fine Thanksgiving dinner. We are going to the Yacht Club tonight for dinner. Should be great.

Lena caught our first fish a few days ago. It was a small tunny (like a tuna). We got two meals out of it. Dark red meat, like beef.

Both Lena and Pender are doing great snorkeling. Pender is working on diving and has gotten about eight feet down. We just got back from Anguilla, which was beautiful. We were unable to go to the classic snorkeling spots because of a large swell from the north, but saw a few beautiful coves on the south side of the island. As we finished dinner on the boat last night, a building we thought was a fish market opened up and turned itself into a very nice restaurant (the "Straw Hat"). We went ashore and said hi. The owner said ours was the first yacht he's seen in the harbor in five years. We wouldn't have been there, but as we were looking for a way into the cove a fisherman came out in his boat and led us into the harbor through a twisted path through the reef and surf.

We saw a cannon underwater while snorkeling in St. Maarten. We've also seen an airplane landing gear, squid, cowfish, puffer fish, grouper, anenome, a ray, a segmented worm, and many types of butterfly fish. We've seen lots of different kinds of coral, but no really healthy reefs, since Hurricane Luis killed most of the coral around here five years ago. The coral does seem to be re-building, though.

The winds here continue to be very light (less than 5 knots). We mostly motored around Anguilla. That makes the beaches nice, and the air hot. The locals think very hot, although at anchor it's not so bad. In town it can be steamy.

Mermaid at anchor in Anguilla.

Weather Conditions

The air and the water are always the same temperature – 82 degrees. Officially, hurricane season is June through November, but the great majority of the storms are in August and September. The sun shines all the time. Gentle breezes keep the islands cool and the bugs away. That's what we heard, that's what we read, and that's what we believed. We found out differently.

The first thing we found out was that we should have brought more fleece and better foul-weather gear. November, especially, was cold. Not cold in a freezing rain and hail sense, but cold in a long pants, long-sleeve shirt, and fleece jacket sense. We still had some warm days and nights, but the cold days really took us by surprise. We had only one set of warm clothes for each of us, and the waterproof windbreakers that came with the boat were entirely inadequate as foul weather gear (and they leaked anyway).

While we were in St. Maarten in November, the breezes shifted west and stayed there for two weeks or so. We thought it was odd, but we were busy getting the boat ready and didn't pay much attention. What we found out later was that many of the locals were very worried about another hurricane like Lenny forming and coming through the island. In November 1999 Lenny formed southwest of Jamaica, then headed east, gaining strength. The category IV hurricane, with sustained winds of 100 knots and gusts of 185 knots, sat right on top of St. Maarten for 24 hours and did an enormous amount of damage.

Our first passage was to Anguilla, a small British island just north of St. Maarten. The wind was from the northwest for most of this two-day trip. On the trip, we saw four water spouts. We'd never seen one before, and we didn't know if they were like tornadoes or more like dust devils. We tracked one for about 30 minutes right before dusk as it came straight toward us, then disappeared when it came close to the island. It re-formed as the storm cell passed the island to the east.

On our earlier trips sailing chartered boats in the BVI, rain squalls were welcome. They'd blow through and you'd get wet and cool off, then quickly warm up again in the following sun. During the early part of this trip, we'd get chilled in a squall and be cold the rest of the day. When we got into a few squalls that lasted for two or three hours, we'd be shivering inside our foul-weather gear.

The sun did shine a lot but most days were partly cloudy with large puffy clouds moving quickly from the east. We had a few days that were mostly overcast.

The "normal" wind in the Caribbean blows from the east at about 10-20 knots. Often in winter, the "Christmas winds" blow for a few weeks at 20-35 knots. These winds result in normal sea states that would be historic in our home waters of Puget Sound. In the Caribbean, a normal sailing day would be 15 to 20-knot winds, 6 to 8-foot seas. When we were in St. Anne on Martinique and the forecast was for 25 to 35-knot winds and 13 to 16-foot seas, we stayed put for a few weeks. We were very surprised at how big 6 to 8-foot seas are. Even in our 40-foot boat, which we considered huge, an eight-foot wave throws you around a little. The occasional 12-foot wave, taken broadside, can be disturbing.

In our home waters of Puget Sound, if you wake up on the boat and it's really raining and there are dark bottom clouds screaming overhead at 50 to 60 miles per hour you leap out of bed and wake the family. After getting everyone dressed in three layers of clothing and rain gear, you start looking into getting somewhere safe and warm before the really bad weather hits. In the Caribbean, it's just another day. I wasted many mornings "anticipating" the cold and wet storm that never came. Squalls blow through and that's the end of it.

We knew that our most reliable weather reports would be over the SSB (Single Side Band) radio. However, we didn't want to go to the expense and trouble of a full SSB installation, which can easily cost over $5,000. Instead, we bought a portable SSB receiver and ran its wire antenna up the port flag halyard. This worked great. We installed We-FAX (Weather FAX) software on one of our laptops and connected the laptop to the SSB receiver. We-FAX is exactly like a FAX machine, but the encoded diagrams are transmitted over SSB radio waves. The system worked great during testing at home, but for some reason we couldn't get it to work on the boat. When we needed weather maps for passages, we downloaded them from the Internet using our Iridium satellite phone connected to a laptop computer.

In the Antilles, we used David Jones' weather forecasts almost exclusively. We would try to catch his AM radio broadcast on ZBVI, then switch over and listen to his more detailed general forecast and customized passage forecasts on the SSB. Some of the islands, such as the Bahamas and Antigua, had very good local weather forecasts. The French islands had great local forecasts on the VHF, but they were in French. We spent an hour or more every day tracking the weather, even on days at anchor. The United States government voice weather radio products were not useful for us. The computer voice on the main SSB stations was often garbled, and the English VHF forecast in Puerto Rico was too heavily accented to understand (and I grew up in New Mexico listening to Spanish accents). We used David Jones' forecasts all though the Virgins until we got to the Bahamas, where he was difficult to pick up. Fortunately, the Bahamas have a great local radio net with news and weather, and you can often pick up Florida radio and TV stations. While we were waiting to cross the Gulf Stream on our way to Ft. Lauderdale we used a small pocket TV to watch local thunderstorm activity on Florida news stations.

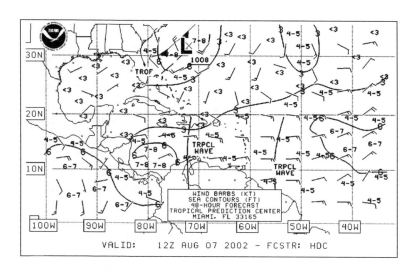

NOAA Wind and Waves Chart

From: Phil, Nancy, Lena and Pender
To: Mermaid Distribution
Email Sent: November 29, 2001

Hello everyone!

It's Thursday morning, 29 November 2001. We're leaving St. Maarten for St. Barts tomorrow morning first thing. So, today we are finishing our provisioning and shopping, filling the gasoil (Diesel) tank, putting the dingy on deck, and getting all ready to go.

The trip is going well. The weather here is great, although a little cool (we are using both a top sheet and a blanket at night since it cools way off to 75 or so). The winds are still very light and out of the North, and there is a large north swell (10-15 feet, supposedly), both caused by the hurricane over Bermuda. No worries for us. The trade winds (from the East, 15-25 knots) should start blowing again in the next little while.

From St. Barts we plan to keep moving approximately south, stair stepping down the islands to Grenada. We don't know whether we'll go south fast, then come north slow, or visa-versa, or what. We'll decide as we see how much we like sailing and what the weather does. Many of the islands south of here are little more than Volcano tops or shallow spots in the sea, so they offer little in the way of safe anchorage.

Phil, Nancy, Pender and Lena

Our routine is fairly established. Nancy has done a good job of laying out the kids' schoolwork, and for the most part they get their work done on time by themselves. Right now they both just finished a spelling test, Lena is finishing an algebra pre-test, and Pender is working on his math.

We got the inverter hooked up and are able to charge all the camera and computer batteries and use the food vacuum packer. It's all pretty civilized. Yesterday we sanded and oiled the teak, so you know we've gotten most of the projects done.

Three pictures are attached so you can remember what we look like. Sorry about the sunglasses. We love getting email and wish we could do a better job replying to them.

We hope you all had a great Thanksgiving and are getting ready for a wonderful Christmas.

Love,
Phil, Nancy, Lena and Pender

Money

Dealing with money was a fun part of our trip. We used U.S. dollars, Eastern Caribbean (EC) dollars, French francs, Dutch guilders, euros and Bahamian dollars. In fact, the euro was introduced while we were in Les Saintes in Guadeloupe. We ran out of francs, they wouldn't take U.S. dollars, and they didn't get the new euros in time, so we couldn't buy anything for a few days.

Most places in the Caribbean take credit cards, but there is almost always a 3% discount for cash. We tried to pay cash whenever we could, and ended up hiding our credit cards for most of the trip. We were able to get cash from ATM machines throughout the islands (in local currency). There were a few times when we needed money faster than we could get it from the machines. For instance, while making repairs in St. Maarten, we could get only $500 per day out of the ATMs, so we repaired things as we could get money. It was theoretically possible to get larger amounts of money directly from the bank, but because of increased security after September 11, the process was a mess and we didn't bother.

Especially in the French islands and the Bahamas there was little customer service or consideration of the consumer. Stores were open at odd and random hours, service was polite but guarded, and the shops were usually run at the convenience of the owner. I actually got to like the system-it looked like a good way to live as a storeowner-but it took a lot of getting used to. One woman in the Bahamas asked me, "Do you really need these stamps? Sometimes people buy stamps and then don't use them, and then we don't have no more stamps!" She was irate. I did need the stamps, and promised to mail some-thing right away.

For souvenirs the kids collected every type of coin we could find. Shop owners had a lot of fun helping them get the more obscure coins, like the EC penny which is just slightly larger than the period at the end of this sentence.

For safety, we tried to go to ATM machines only during the daytime, limited the cash we carried, and kept our heads up and our eyes open while walking around.

We had both a secret and a not-so-secret money stash on the boat, as suggested by several experienced cruisers. We kept a large emergency fund vacuum-sealed and well-hidden for real emergencies. We also kept about $300 poorly hidden, so that if someone did break into our boat they would find that money and leave.

Our sister-in-law helped us enormously by paying our personal bills and answering our mail while we were gone. We might have been able to pay all our bills on-line, but having her check through our mail and keep the bills paid helped us a lot. We didn't have mail forwarded, but when we had visitors they delivered some of our personal mail.

Under normal global/economic circumstances, the largest and possibly the only cost of the trip would have been the lost income from being away from our business. We had a house sitter who took care of our house and paid the house bills. Our daily living expenses, excluding the boat purchase and outfitting, were less than we spent at home because we lived simply and didn't have to put gas in the car. The boat was worth so much more in the States than it was down-island that it would have more than paid for itself and our improvements if not for the terrorist attack between the time we bought the boat and returned her to Seattle. Because of the terrorist attacks, it's more difficult to sell the boat now and the value may be lower than when we bought it.

From: Phil, Nancy, Lena and Pender
To: Mermaid Distribution
Email Sent: December 7, 2001

Hello, all, from Nevis, the southern island of St. Kitts (aka St. Christopher).

This will be a short message because we are sending it by satellite phone. We wanted to get a good weather report, so we thought we would send a short email as well.

St. Kitts has been very educational for us. They are not set up very well to receive and take care of yachts. To clear in to customs, you tie up to a rope or rebar sticking out of a riprap wall. To get dinghy gas, you walk 1/2 to one mile with the gas can to a Shell station (6 gallons of gas weighs only 36 pounds, but feels like much more). To go see the sights, you pick out a cabby you want to work with, then negotiate the trip and cost. After you have agreed upon the package, he takes you to his good friend who will take care of you, and you repeat the process. The second man finally takes you to his good friend, you repeat the process, and you go sightseeing. Luckily, our driver turned out to be a very good guide and we learned a lot about the island. I guess the moral of the story is that there is a system, but it's their system. Really, everything has worked out really well on the trip so far, but the process of getting things done has been stressful for us.

We are quickly becoming sailors. On the sail from St. Barts to St. Kitts we averaged 6.5 knots, with a max speed (GPS) of 10 knots. I think the max speed was a short burst surfing down a wave. We sailed through our second major storm. Squalls are common, where it gets windy (30 knots) and very rainy for a short time. We have sailed through two storms with the same conditions for 45 minutes. Last night, after a restaurant dinner in St. Kitts (at Stonewalls, a famous place and great) we sailed for over an hour in the dark and then anchored in a quiet cove. We felt very "salty."

Tomorrow we will sail from here to Antigua to meet some friends at a boat show. That will be a 42-mile sail, directly into the wind. Should be fun. I think we will spend a fair amount of time in Antigua and Barbuda just hanging around. Apparently they have some nice beaches and coral there.

The picture attached is of the kids at Fort Charles, the giant restored English fort on Brimstone Hill on St. Kitts. Brimstone Hill is a magma intrusion through a limestone formation, so the fort is made of andesite (cooled lava) blocks cemented together with mortar made from limestone, all collected right on the site. You can smell sulfur as you drive up to the fort, so obviously there is some volcanic stuff still going on.

Lena and Pender at Brimstone Hill on St. Kitts.

We have heard most of the news while waiting to hear weather reports on local radio, so it sounds like things are well. We hope you are all enjoying getting ready for Christmas. The kids made 25 paper snowflakes and raindrops and put them up in the cabin, and we have a string of lights. Very festive. We do appreciate the weather reports from home and London letting us know what we're missing. We also appreciate all the Iridium messages. I wish we could answer them personally. I do hope to spend an hour or so at an Internet cafe and answer some of the email before Christmas.

All our love:

Phil, Nancy, Lena and Pender

From: Phil, Nancy, Lena and Pender
To: Mermaid Distribution
Email Sent: December 25, 2001

Merry Christmas and Happy New Year!

We let the kids write this one.

Dear everyone:

I am doing fine, here in Antigua. So far I'm the dinghy captain, a great snorkeler, and have reverse seasickness. Here are what we mostly do every day: get up at 7:00, have breakfast, listen to the weather, do school, have lunch, explore, have dinner, then either we play cards or we read or we do both.

If you're wondering what a dinghy captain is it's a person who ties, clips, and cleats rope; he, she would also get the dinghy ready to be driven. If you are also wondering what reverse seasickness is, well regular seasickness only affects you when you're inside of the boat instead it affects me only when I go outside of the boat. Just recently we all saw 4 dolphins 3 were grownups, one was a baby. Merry Christmas and a Happy New Year!

From: Pender

Hey how's it going everyone? So far it really fun here in Antigua. Hope you all have a great Christmas and a groovy New Year. We put in the Christmas CDs yesterday. Snorkeling is ok (I'm not very interested in snorkeling). I'm more interested in finding cool colored shells; so far I have found a hand full of purple and bright pink shells. I also found an old piece of pottery in the surf, it's about 100 years old. School is ok it takes about 2 to 2½ hours every morning. I already started science and am ahead in all of my other classes. I'm running out of books to read because I read 4 or more a week. We are playing a lot of card games like rummy or solitaire. There is a game here called warri it is kind of like mancala. We go to a lot of museums (there is about one museum on each island). We went to an art studio where the lady paints on silk. Yesterday we saw 4 dolphins.

From: Lena

We'll let the kids do the talking for this message. The kids put up paper snowflakes and raindrops, and we have a very small fir tree branch for smelling. The rain should stop today or tomorrow. We'll head south after Christmas.

Merry Christmas to all of you.

Phil and Nancy

Merry Christmas from Mermaid!

Documenting the Trip

We knew we would be making a video of the trip. Any cruiser can use the same equipment to document their cruise and make an amazingly good video to remember the trip. The quality available in consumer cameras and editing equipment today was available only to professionals just a few years ago. Our video is available at www.caribmermaid.com.

Our video camera was a Sony Digital8 Handycam. Professionals and network news photographers use the DV (Digital Video) format all over the world. You can directly import the DV into a modern laptop computer using a Firewire port. Once the video is inside the computer, specialized programs let you edit the video and transform it into any project you want. We took hundreds of hours of video, which we then roughly culled and saved onto 123 CDs, each holding about three minutes of video. We transferred all the video to CD so that the pictures weren't lost if the tapes mildewed or were erased by an airport x-ray machine.

We used Fisheye underwater video cameras to take video underwater. These cameras transmit the video to a camcorder above the surface for viewing and recording. You can dive or snorkel with the underwater camera head, or you can just dangle it from your boat or dinghy while you drift over an area.

For still photographs we used a Sony Mavica digital camera and an Olympus 35 MM "point and shoot" film camera. We tried to take really good care of both cameras, but the Olympus was broken late in the trip. We did not take a good 35 MM SLR camera. We figured the sand and water would kill it.

For underwater still pictures we used an Ikelite Aquashot housing. You use disposable cameras inside this housing, so if (when) the housing leaks, you don't lose anything of value. The real key to using the Ikelite housing is to buy the strobe accessory. The added light from the strobe really adds to the color and vibrancy of your pictures. We brought rechargeable batteries for the strobe.

We also used disposable underwater cameras for snorkeling pictures. They worked fine for shallow shots. Standard disposable cameras were great to take to the beach and town. The pictures are very good, and we didn't have to spend a lot of time keeping the cameras clean and dry. For the most part, we developed pictures along the way when we found a one-hour developing place. Developing quality was always good.

Because you need specific cameras to use in the underwater housing, we brought a lot of these cameras with us. We were also able to find disposable cameras, 35 mm film and blank CDs in the islands, although it wasn't always easy.

I had some experience with photography and videography, and I wish I had spent more time before the trip teaching Nancy and the kids how to frame pictures and hold the camera still to get good video shots, but they were all doing great by the end of the trip.

Nancy, Lena and Pender all kept journals. I wrote most of the emails, so I didn't keep a separate journal.

From: Phil, Nancy, Lena and Pender
To: Mermaid Distribution
Email Sent: January 2, 2002

Happy New Year to everyone!

Announcing the first annual "Where the heck are they?" contest. We are at 15 degrees, 51.7 minutes north; 61 degrees, 36.0 minutes west. The first three replies to the following email address will receive a post card from that place.

Send your entries to:

8816XXXXXXXX@msg.iridium.com

Include the island or town name, your name, your mailing address, and what type of postcard you want (beach babe, beach boy, beach, inland picture, or food). Remember that you can send only 120 characters to this address, including the spaces. If you want, leave the spaces out and we'll figure it out.

Extra credit: If we buy bread here, what words do we use?

We are having a very interesting time in the French islands. The French have done a much better job integrating their societies, so there is much less racial segregation/tension in the French islands. Also the roads are better. We wonder if they spend more money in their islands than other countries, or just do a better job. Also, the beaches are better in the French islands. I'm not sure why, I just like them more. Hmmm.

Pender got a boogie board for Christmas. It's a soft surfboard thing that you lie on to go bodysurfing. We went to an incredibly beautiful gold-sand beach on Guadeloupe and all went bodysurfing and boogie boarding. Pender and I were playing in the waves just outside the rollers. Then a big breaking wave came though and wiped us both out, holding us both under and smashing my head into his teeth. My head is fine, thanks for asking. Pender has a fat lip. Pender will not go into the water with me now.

Nancy and I finally went scuba diving. The water here is 80 degrees and you don't need a wetsuit (or any suit, really). Nancy and I wear "skins," which are like full-length swimsuits with arms and legs. Nancy's has a pink racing stripe and mine has a red racing stripe. There is a marine park, founded by Cousteau, with lots of cool diving. Truly a great place with lots of fish, corals and sponges. In fact, there were so many fish in this marine park that the locals fish there using seine nets, and the local game fishing boats stop off to jig for bait on their way out in the morning. It's amazing what you learn if you wake up early enough.

Pender and Lena are collecting coins from each island. They are especially excited about the new euro coins being introduced tomorrow. Pender wants to get a full euro collection from each country (they are like the state quarters, with each coin being issued separately from each participating country).

Lena is really concentrating on fishing, although we have had very little luck. She has a lot of fun at night shining the spotlight into the water and seeing what comes to eat the plankton that gathers. Last night we had three small squid (about 2 inches long) that hung around for a while. Very cool.

Nancy's 40th birthday is tomorrow. We're not sure what we'll do, or where we'll be. Somehow, chocolate will be involved.

If you are in or near New York, the boat show opens this Friday. Enjoy.

Have a great New Year!

Love,

Phil, Nancy, Lena and Pender Rink

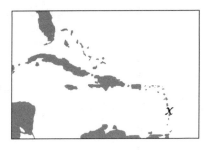

From: Phil, Nancy, Lena and Pender
To: Mermaid Distribution
Email Sent: January 11, 2002

Hello:

The winners of last message's contest will soon be getting their awards. The people who answered wrong will get a booby prize of some sort. The people who didn't answer, or answered but didn't give an address (Herb) or answered and didn't leave their name (two people) get nothing. Nothing. Not a thing. Seems sad. There were five people who correctly identified that we were in "Iles des Saintes," a group of islands south of the main island of Guadeloupe that, like Guadeloupe, are actually a part of France. They are not a territory, or a protectorate, or anything, but a state. Kind of cool.

For the extra credit, bread in France is "pain," pronounced "pain". We buy "baguettes" and go through one loaf (about 0,5m to 1,0 m long) per day. That's why bread is a pain, you are always looking for a Boulangerie/ Patisserie to buy more bread. Usually, you need to find the cash machine first. That's usually at "La Poste," which is also where they hand out the social security $$$, and is always crowded. We are now spending euros here in France. Verrrry cosmopolitan!

So, today was a big day for the Rinks. We sailed from Marie Galante (another island in the south of Guadeloupe) to St. Pierre at the north end of Martinique. We sailed right by Dominica (say: "NI!" the loudest). That made for a 14-hour sailing day from anchor/anchor. Since the trade winds are unusually light at 5-10 knots, the seas were fairly calm, but our own boat speed meant we were sailing into the wind all day instead of on a broad reach (across the wind) like we anticipated. All in all, the trip went really well. It was extremely scary to raise anchor and leave at 3:30 a.m. in the dark. Luckily we didn't hit a squall (violent rain and wind storm common in the Caribbean) until dawn and we could see it coming. When it finally stopped raining and the sun came up, we found two small flying fish on deck. They were incredibly beautiful. One of them died with a very sur- prised look on its face.

Lena and Nancy enjoyed shopping in Guadeloupe for French clothes. On the boat, Nancy has gone almost completely native, wearing pareos most of the time. A pareo is a brightly printed piece of cloth that you can tie in various ways to almost cover yourself. Phil wears jogging shorts and little else except when going to visit the customs officer.

We visited a sugar cane grinding windmill, and although nobody there spoke any English, had a great time. The guide cut us open some cane to taste (it was great), then gave us some more cane to take home. None of the French people got any cane. It's good to be the pathetic tourist.

We are in search of the perfect beach here in Martinique. It will be very hard to beat "Grand Anse" on Guadeloupe. Grand Anse was probably a mile long, filled with coarse light golden sand. A very light surf gave us lots of waves to play in. We will keep searching, and report back as required.

St. Pierre, the town we are in tonight, was killed by a volcano in 1903. The mayor was amply warned, but refused to evacuate the town so all 33,000 residents were killed except for a killer in the jail and a store owner in his cellar. No word whether the mayor left town. We will go ashore tomorrow and see the sights.

That seems like enough for now. Let us know if you want us to talk about things that we haven't covered.

Love,

Phil, Nancy, Lena and Pender Rink

Making Passages

Before this trip, Nancy and I had never sailed a sailboat longer than 14 feet without a more experienced person on board. The biggest sailboat either of us had ever owned was carried on the roof of my 1972 Vega while I was in college in New Mexico.

Because *Mermaid* was an easy boat to sail, because we didn't let our schedule make our decisions for us, and because we were extremely conservative, we had a great time and proved to be more than qualified. The large seas in the open water were at first terrifying, but we persisted and tried to follow the advice of Bruce Van Sant in "The Gentleman's Guide to Passages South" to use the Beaufort scale to determine whether to leave port. If you will have Force 0-2 on the nose, Force 3 close hauled, Force 4 reaching, Force 5 broad reaching, or Force 6 behind you, you will have a nice sail. Otherwise, stay in port and wait. Quoting Bruce: "Force 5 forward of the beam is for the jocks in their yellow slickers eating cold beans from cans." Not for families sailing their house. The Beaufort scale is a way of determining the severity of the weather based on the wave size and wind speed. Force 5 is 17 to 21-knot winds with 6 to 8-foot seas.

While sailing it is very important that one person be the captain, and the rest be crew. There are times to discuss the options and choose a best course. There are times to whine about whether everyone is doing his or her fair share. A jibe in 20 knots of wind and 10-foot seas is not that time. Reefing sails in a squall is not that time. We took turns being captain, but I ended up with the duty more often than I wanted.

We did not keep a set watch schedule while on passage, but we were clear with each other to make sure that someone was paying attention and responsible for the boat at all times. Lena and Pender were very good and trustworthy on watch. We never left them alone in the cockpit in anything but the smoothest weather and only then if they were clipped in with a safety lanyard and harness. On our few overnight passages Nancy and I would take turns sleeping on the cockpit floor while the other drove, so we would not have to go below to wake each other if there was a problem.

We caused some problems for ourselves on passages by being too conservative about daylight and weather. Especially in December and January, we would wait and wait for the wind to ease, often waiting until the wind went almost calm. Then we would end up motor sailing to increase our speed so that we would reach our destination before dark. Other boats would sail easier at night, sailing slower and using smaller sails to keep their trip calmer and then anchor the next morning after dawn. Because we didn't want to sail at night we would drive the boat hard to make some passages in the 12 hours of daylight. If we had left earlier in the morning while it was still dark, or perhaps sailed in slightly stronger winds, we would actually have had easier passages.

Once we turned north from Martinique, however, we started sailing more on broad reaches and runs. Wow. The wind seemed lighter, the air was warmer, and the motion of the boat was much easier. Attitudes improved drastically on downwind sails.

Mermaid's autopilot steered the boat most of the time. The autopilot has its own compass and would steer a truer course than we could by hand. We also connected it to the GPS, so the GPS could correct for drift and currents along the way. When steering by the GPS, sometimes the boat would make large course corrections, spilling wind from the sails and causing general anguish and despair, so we generally used the autopilot to sail by a compass course so we could trim the sails accordingly. We then used the GPS to track our progress against our route, often simply staying offshore of the direct course. In very rough seas or following seas it was smoother to steer by hand, driving around the bigger waves. Nancy would often steer by hand "just because."

Our worst passage was early in the trip from Nevis to Antigua. All the guidebooks tell you not to make this passage. They recommend that you sail from Nevis to Guadeloupe, then Guadeloupe to Antigua. We were (stupidly) in a little bit of a hurry to meet friends in Antigua, and we had some unfounded trepidation about entering customs on a French island, so we tried to sail the route direct. Actually, we tried to sail the route direct for a while. We tacked upwind, bashing into the eight-foot seas and the 20-knot trade winds with the spray and pitching keeping us pinned in the cockpit. The ETA (Estimated Time of Arrival) feature on the GPS showed us that we wouldn't make land until 10 or 11 p.m. So we sailed into the lee of Antigua and motored the final 15 or 20 miles directly into the wind. The ride was even rougher motoring, with the sea crashing over the bow, but at least we were making progress and would be in Falmouth Harbor well before dark. We crawled our way into the calm lee of the island and found that our anchor had broken loose from the bow roller and scratched the crap out of the bow, even punching a small hole in the hull.

After that we made two small changes in our sailing plans. We always tied the anchor down using two separate ties, and we never tried to sail to weather again. We would put out a little mainsail and sheet it in tight-just enough sail to lean us over a little–then motorsail upwind, tacking just enough to keep wind in the mainsail. This technique kept the boat level and reduced pitching. Even motoring slowly we made more headway than if we tried to tack upwind.

Navigating through the Caribbean and Bahamas should not be taken lightly, but it's not all that difficult. There are lots of boats sailing between the islands that may or may not have even a working compass on board. We used two navigational techniques and often compared them with each other. First, we kept the relevant chart handy and constantly compared visual landmarks. Since you can usually see your destination island before you lose sight of the island you are leaving, this technique works great for inter-island navigation. We used binoculars with an integral compass to take headings and triangulate our position. Second, we used GPS equipment to establish and track our position and course. Modern GPS equipment is reliable and incredibly easy to use. We carried three—one built into the boat and integrated with the autopilot, one hand-held that was stored in the cabin, and one hand-held that was stored with the life raft. If there was any lightning in the area we would store one or both of the hand-helds in a metal saucepan with a lid. The metal enclosure would protect the sensitive electronics from damage if we were struck by lightning. The built-in GPS and one of the hand-helds, both from Garmin, had internal maps that made them easy to use. At one point in mid-ocean, we got out one of the hand-helds and set it on the helm to compare to the built-in GPS. They differed by one-thousandth of a minute in latitude, and were exactly the same in longitude. We were amazed. Then we noticed that the antenna for the built-in GPS was on the stern rail, about four feet away. We placed the hand-held next to the fixed antenna, and the displays matched exactly.

The GPS was most useful when traveling down the side of an island. We'd stay a mile or two offshore in deep water until we were at the latitude of our harbor, then turn and drive right in. Most of the islands have rough terrain and very few landmarks, and the harbors were not easy to recognize from a distance.

In-shore navigation is very different in the Caribbean than in our home waters. The navigation aids are often missing or wrong, and it's often necessary to look into the water to see rocks or shallow spots. It's not difficult to navigate by sight in the clear water as long as the sun is high, and preferably over your shoulder.

From: Phil, Nancy, Lena and Pender
To: Mermaid Distribution
Email Sent: January 21, 2002

Hello, all.

We are anchored right off the beach in St. Anne, Martinique. Front row! This is a great, long beach with clear, calm water and white, clean sand. It is busy enough to have tourist facilities, but never crowded or noisy. There is easy and good snorkeling nearby. Yesterday we saw a school of a dozen reef squid, all about 12 inches long, and a smaller school of much smaller squid, all about 1.5 inches long. Nancy and I will probably go diving on a supposedly great reef a short dinghy ride away.

There is a Club Med at the end of the beach. We can walk the beach as far as we want to, although we can't use the facilities. Too bad for us. The on-the-beach massages look pretty good. If any of you are looking for a vacation, the place does not look crowded during what must be their peak season. I imagine the rates are pretty cheap right now.

After finishing their schoolwork for the day, Pender and Lena load stuff into their inflatable kayak and paddle into the beach to play until the afternoon. Pender is now the master of the sand castle, and Lena just has a good time in general. She bought herself a French bikini, so she can fit in with the crowds.

Speaking of beaches, there is something going on down here that you should all know about. French beaches (such as found on St. Martin, Guadeloupe, and Martinique) are, of course, topless. We have all gotten used to that and it is, of course, great. However, something else happens that is quite extraordinary, yet, if you think about it, quite natural. Most of the more populated beaches have vendors of various kinds that sell pastries, sand-wiches, handmade jewelry, coconut crafts, and the like. They also have what we on *Mermaid* call the "Beach Ladies". The Beach Ladies sell swimsuits. Nice swimsuits, often with matching covers or pareos to wear with the suits. They carry large woven baskets full of suits and accessories so that the customers can find one that fits their needs. So far, so good. Well, these young businesswomen often find themselves without customers and need to advertise their suits and attract attention. Assuming that her current suit is not attractive to the people nearby, the Beach Lady will simply spread a blanket in the sand in front of a likely looking crowd and start changing her suit! She will change out of one, and into another, then out of that suit, into a third, etc. Quite astonishing. They never actually get naked, since they are wearing a thong under all the "sale" suits. (I haven't seen one yet lose track and take the bottom suit off!) (Not that I'm looking.) Now, here is the weird part: Women of all sizes, ages, and shapes will notice what the Beach Ladies are doing, come up and look through their wares, then start trying on suits themselves! Actually, it all seems fairly normal here. But when I think of the same thing happening at Green Lake in Seattle, or Lake Wawasee in Indiana, or Lake Michigan, or, God help us, LAKE COCHITI in New Mexico, I just need to lie down for a while. Nancy has not yet bought a suit from the Beach Ladies. Lena looked into it, but they didn't have her size.

Incidentally, there are "Beach Men." Nobody wants to know what they do.

We are pinned down at this beach by the "Christmas winds." Maybe we're being too cautious, but 9 to 12-foot seas with 25-knot sustained winds seems like big stuff. We'll wait here until they lay down for a while (which will be another week) before heading back north. Actually, we would like to get some email from those of you out there who have actually been in such stuff to know if we should just go ahead and leave. Those of you who haven't been in it but want us to go anyway, thanks for your good thoughts. The winds at the beach itself are actually much lighter, but are up around 20 knots at night. We are seeing a very slight swell, but barely enough for the kids to go boogie boarding.

There is a football/handball field right next to the beach. So far we've caught the last five minutes of a handball game and the last three minutes of a football (soccer) game. We need to find a schedule, and then translate the schedule into English. For now we just listen for the ref whistles, then jump into the dinghy, go to the beach, and try and catch the game.

Pender has also gone native, and often wears a pareo. His hair has turned gold in the sunlight, and his skin is very tan. He looks like the island poster boy. Since he is spending so much time in the water, he asked Nancy for swimming lessons and is becoming a good swimmer.

Someone stopped Nancy and Lena in town and asked them (in French) for directions to the bank. Oddly enough, they were able to help.

I hope the euro changeover is going well for you all, and that the stores and banks have all adjusted.

Have a good winter.

Phil, Nancy, Lena and Pender

Meeting and Making Friends

Story 1.

We went ashore in St. Pierre, Martinique, to see the town that had been buried by a volcano and visit a rum factory in the surrounding hills. We had been in the French islands for some time and had not spoken much English except to each other. While walking through the town, we heard a couple speaking English-England English. We stopped to ask them for directions and did they know where the customs office was? They did not know any more than we did about St. Pierre, but once the woman found out I was American she made sure I knew that she was furious that the Taliban prisoners were being kept at Guantanamo Bay in Cuba. They had hoped to stop there and now it wouldn't be safe. I smiled, then frowned, then sighed. I finally asked her where in England would she like us to send them? She explained to me that England had more than their share of those people, thank you. We bid them farewell and moved on.

Soon afterward we came across a family of four. The father of the other family and I greeted each other with a loud: "Howdy!" Americans! We talked for a short while, learned each other's (first) names, and talked about having a beer later on their boat. Where to meet with new friends and share a beer is a very common topic of conversation in the Caribbean. Great! We asked if their kids, roughly the same age as Lena and Pender, would like to join us on a hike to the rum factory, letting their parents have a little private time. And off we went. We were gone about three hours, walking up into the foothills, around the grounds of the ancient factory, and back down to the beach on another road. Their kids and ours were polite and adventurous and got along great. When we got back to the beach, their dad swooped ashore in their dinghy, very happy to see his kids again. "I suppose we should have learned each other's last names and boat names before we sent our kids off with you," he said. I suppose he was right, but it honestly felt fine and normal to feel that safe around strangers. We made great friends with the crew of *TIME* from Beaufort, South Carolina, and our paths crossed many times after that. Please, at all times, remember that Beaufort, South Carolina, is pronounced like beautiful.

Story 2.

Les Saintes is a small archipelago south of the main island of Guadeloupe with a very small permanent population and a large number of tourists, both cruisers and ferry travelers from "mainland" Guadeloupe. We had stopped there on our way south and loved it, so we stopped again on our way back north and anchored just south of "Pain de Sucre," a small volcanic mountain in the middle of the main island. We had been in the French islands for about two months by this time, and were very comfortable with their customs and rhythms. Nancy and I decided to go scuba diving just north of the anchorage, so we anchored the dinghy and left the kids at the small swimming beach at the foot of the rocks.

Nancy and I had a beautiful dive and saw many colorful fish along with the ubiquitous fish traps. We surfaced and swam back to the dinghy, where we left our tanks and backpacks and stripped off our full-body swimsuits. Nancy and I were both topless. We swam in to the beach and lay in the sun, letting the kids play in the water.

Lena and Pender both came over to us and whispered: "There's another family here from Seattle!"

"Well, go say hi!" I said.

"You come too, we're afraid!"

"Mom and I are going to lie in the sun and warm up. You go say hi!"

"Come on, Dad."

So we met the other family from Seattle. They were also cruising with their son, Pender's age, and two younger girls, and they introduced us to a family from Detroit. The family from Detroit had three pre-teen boys and had been out for some time.   We all sat in the shallow water and talked about sailing and kids and sailboats and beaches and school and life on a boat and shopping and so forth. I was starting to get cold, and I noticed that Nancy was kind of hunkered down in the water. Oops. Sure enough, Nancy had noticed that she was topless and the other women weren't. What had seemed so natural was suddenly out of place. To their credit, the other couples didn't act at all uncomfortable, and the kids certainly didn't care. However, Nancy, our kids and I retreated to Mermaid, where we all put shirts on and later met both families for cocktails and more talk about kids and school and sailboats and beaches and …..

Again, we became good friends with the families from *Simpatica* (from Seattle) and *Ti Malou* (from Detroit) and met up with them again often on our way north and east.

Lena and Nancy boogie boarding at Grand Anse, Guadeloupe.

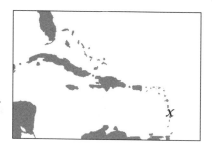

From: Phil, Nancy, Lena and Pender
To: Mermaid Distribution
Email Sent: January 23, 2002

Some people have asked for more stuff on the boring day-to-day that goes on here. Since we are stuck in St. Anne in Martinique, we have nothing but day-to-day going on. Here is some boring information, as opposed to the other stuff we've written, which was not boring.

The boat has three cabins. Mom and Dad sleep up front, and Pender and Lena each have their own cabin at the back of the boat, under the cockpit. At anchor, it is usually cool enough to sleep well with only a small hatch in the front of the boat cracked open, and a hatch in each of the kids' cabins open for flow-through ventilation. Despite being about 1,000 miles east of Florida, all of the Caribbean islands are on Atlantic Standard Time. This means that the sun sets at 5:30 in the evening, and it's dark by 6. We usually go to bed at 8:30 or 9, read for a short time, then go right to sleep. The kids sleep straight through to 7 or 8, while Mom and Dad are usually up once or twice to check on weird noises and open/close hatches as rain squalls come through. Everyone gets their own breakfast, usually cereal, then we all need to be really quiet for the weather on the Single Side Band (SSB) radio at 8:30 a.m. After the weather, we run the boat engine for one hour to make the refrigerator/freezer cold, and also charge the batteries. The engine is pretty loud in the boat and makes it uncomfortable, but we need to run it sometime. If we run it in the morning, it (and the boat) is usually cooled off by night-time. We usually run the watermaker during this time, also. The watermaker "strains" the salt out of the seawater to make fresh water. In one hour, we make 4-5 gallons of fresh water, which we use for all our drinking, cooking, and washing.

After the weather, the kids do their schoolwork and Mom and Dad read, help with school, work on the boat, or find something else to do. Sometimes Mom and Dad go snorkeling during this time. The kids usually finish their schoolwork by lunchtime. They are both doing well in math and OK in spelling. Other subjects are difficult for both them and us, although we are finding ways to cover science, writing, and geography, and, for Lena, music. We then eat lunch (sandwiches or something hot from a can), then go to the beach or to town for the afternoon. When we get back to the boat, we all use fresh water to rinse off the salt. Sometimes we take baths in the ocean before rinsing off with fresh water. Even in a crowded anchorage, this is no big deal. Everyone else does the same thing, so nobody stares. Sometimes it's a little weird when you are anchored right off shore in front of a housing complex or something, but you can always wait until after dark to bathe.

Lena and Mom usually cook supper, although Dad and Pender have both cooked a few meals. Suppers have been great. We have a two-burner stove with oven and broiler that runs off propane. We also have a propane barbecue that hangs off the stern rail that we use to cook hamburgers, pork chops, and chicken. We cook food that's about the same as we cooked at home, although we are more careful about not using so many pots and pans, and we use slightly fewer ingredients. The only food that we've really had trouble finding is corn and flour tortillas. We've been making burritos with Vietnamese rice paper tortillas. They are actually very good, and very tough and easy to use.

We have a wind generator to help charge the batteries. We call it the noise generator, since noise is its principal product. We had high hopes for it, but except for very windy days (15-20 knots) it's pretty useless and very loud.

We very rarely use sunscreen anymore, although we try to put it on if we are going to go to the beach for a long time. We used quite a bit of sunscreen when we first got here, and everyone tanned evenly. Nobody even peeled much. The cockpit of the boat has a Bimini, which is like a tarp cover, but we usually leave it stowed so we get the most light and sun. The cabin of the boat has only small windows and portlights, so it's almost always cool and shaded below as long as there is a little air moving through. Rain squalls come through about four times a day, dumping about 1/8 to 1/4 inch of rain in 15 minutes, so we also close the boat up tight when we leave. It cools off within about 10 minutes when we get back and open it up.

We (mostly Nancy) do laundry once a week or so in a bucket at the back of the boat. She washes and rinses the clothes in salt water, then rinses them again in fresh water and hangs them up to dry in the rigging and on the lifelines. We've found that the T-shirts we brought from home all fit loosely because we don't have the heat of a dryer to shrink them up every time. Mostly we've gone to wearing nylon shorts and tops because cotton gets a little salt water on it and then never dries out.

We have not eaten a fish we've caught since we got here, except for a tunny that Lena caught in Anguilla in December. There are three reasons for this. First of all, we haven't caught many fish. There is a (huge) chance that we don't know what we're doing. We are getting better, though, we think. We have lost some very expensive lures to some very large fish, but you can't eat stories. The second reason that we aren't eating fish is that the reefs around the islands we've been to are grossly over-fished. They fish with traps, and the traps usually catch very few, very small fish in the reefs we snorkel. When we do see areas with fish, we don't want to spearfish or lure fish because we want the area to recover. The third reason we haven't been catching a lot of fish is that there is a neurological disease called ciguatera that you get from eating certain reef fish that have ingested a toxic bacteria. The bacteria is impossible to detect, and you might not get sick right away, but when you do get sick you are sick for a long time, perhaps for the rest of your life. All in all, chicken sounds good. We would like to catch a nice dolphin (Dorado) or wahoo on an inter-island passage, however.

The "toilets" on the boat are simple marine heads that pump the waste directly overboard. Mermaid has holding tanks for both heads, but there are no pump-out facilities in the Caribbean, so a full waste tank would be a disaster. In fact, I think there is some liquid in the aft holding tank. No telling how long it's been there or what's in it. Despite the fact that all boats here are equipped this way, and some of the anchorages are really crowded, you don't hear about outbreaks of dysentery or other disease. My feeling is that seawater has an enormous capacity for organic material. A bigger problem are areas like the lagoon in St. Maarten, which not only receives the boat waste but also the sewage from surrounding houses. The water in the lagoon does not exchange very often. We don't swim or run the watermaker there. The sinks in the heads and kitchen also drain directly overboard.

When we want to go ashore, we take our dinghy. We have a 10 1/2-foot inflatable dinghy with a fiberglass bottom and a 15-hp outboard motor. It is very fast, maybe 20 mph. It's really fun to take it out in the big ocean. Also scary and stupid. When we are sailing locally, we just drag the dinghy behind us on a 50-foot rope. Sometimes we go through big seas and the dinghy jumps right into the air. When we are cruising between islands, we put the outboard on a bracket at the stern of Mermaid (on the "push-pit") and use a halyard (line from the top of the mast that we use to pull up the sails) to lift the dinghy and put it on the deck in front of the mast. We then tie the dinghy down really well so it doesn't blow overboard. The kids also have an inflatable canoe that they can use in calm harbors to paddle around and go to the beach.

We have met only one other family cruising with their kids. They were from South Carolina, and they left in June and cruised around during hurricane season. They have had their boat for years, and had been offshore before, so both the kids and parents were seasoned boaters and thought nothing of going on multi-week offshore passages. We are still sweating whether we should try an overnight. However, we were able to swap books, so that was great. It turns out they knew Pat Conroy, and I had just finished "The Great Santini." Pretty cool.

We have averaged $50/day living expenses since we left St. Maarten, counting everything except the Iridium bill that may be very high. That's about what we hoped to do. Eating ashore has been a mixed bag. We have had some great meals. The other night, I ordered "brochettes" de something or other, which I knew was shishkabob. What came was indeed barbecued skewers of meat. The meat was completely unidentifiable. I didn't know if I was eating pig cartilage, cow kneecaps, ox tails bits, or what. It turns out that they were some kind of seasnail (not conch) or scallop or oyster or whatever. That was an adventure. Once I knew it was seafood, it tasted a little better. To top it all off, Lena's crepe had bell peppers (red and green) in it, so it was completely inedible.

Our first guests will be meeting us in St. Maarten from Seattle the week after Valentine's Day. We are looking forward to seeing them. If you want to come down (and if you received this message, you are certainly invited) give us a date and we'll tell you where we'll be, as best we can.

Note on Sending Messages to the Iridium Phone:

The Iridium Phone is a great way to send us short messages. However, messages are limited to 120 characters, including all spaces and headings, so it is very important to count characters before you send. As an example, we received the following, tragic message after our last letter. Remember that we had asked for opinions as to whether we should go sailing even if the wind was 25 knots with 12-foot seas: "Dear All: I really love your messages and am glad you are all well and happy. For what it's worth, I would vote that you." As with the Florida butterfly ballots, that vote went un-recorded. When sending messages to the iridium phone, you can eliminate spaces, punctuation, and salutations. We'll figure it out. We love to get these messages, even when we don't know whom they're from or what they are trying to say.

Bon jour:

Phil, Nancy, Lena and Pender

Health and Safety

We worried a lot about it before we left home, but the truth is that we have never been healthier than we were on this trip. Nobody got sick, no one had allergies or hay fever, no food poisoning, and very little seasickness. Lena and Pender grew like crazy. Nancy and I lost weight we didn't even know we were carrying.

Before we left home, Nancy and I went to the tanning booths and got deeply tanned. At home in the Pacific Northwest, a good summer tan just barely darkens you. Our kids had never had a dark tan or sunburn in their lives. The kids couldn't go in the tanning booths before we left, so they had to be really careful when we got to St. Maarten. We kept them covered in SPF-40 sunscreen for about two weeks or so, then gradually let them get more and more sun. They never burned, had very little peeling, and within a month or so we rarely used sunscreen unless we really felt we needed it, like if we were going to the beach for the day. I did get a bad burn on my nose that took a month or so to heal. I spent so much of my childhood with blistering sunburns that I doubt I did any additional damage to my skin.

We had learned that the dangerous parasites and diseases in the tropics are mostly associated with fresh water. Because of this, we stayed away from streams and puddles and usually didn't go inland. We know we missed some great things because of this, but we never really felt as if we missed out. We did meet a man in Antigua who was just getting over dengue fever. His condition (thin and drawn) made our over-precautions seem worthwhile. We always wore shoes or sandals when walking inland further than the beach so we didn't get parasites that live in the mud.

Easily the most dangerous activity on the trip was walking near the island traffic. Some islanders drive on the right, some islanders drive on the left, many pick and choose trying to avoid the larger potholes. Most island drivers are very courteous and cautious, but we had enough near misses to keep us wary.

Stress is self-imposed and self-moderated. You can always find things to be stressed about, if that is your nature. Both Nancy and I found plenty to be stressed about. Once or twice a week arguing with the kids over schoolwork started everyone's day with a good blast of adrenaline. We were usually in an anchorage for three to four days, so the first night we'd decompress from the passage and wonder if our anchor was going to hold. The last night we'd worry about the passage we were going to make the next day. There was usually some bad weather or difficulty finding food on the one or two days in between, and we always needed to keep an eye on how skillfully our neighbors anchored. At least once every night one of us would wake up to check on things. Talking to other cruisers, the number one negative comment was that you could never relax completely. There was always some terrible crisis just over the horizon. On a future trip back to the islands, we would now recognize that many of the things we worried about were not worth the trouble, and we would also have more confidence in our boat and our abilities.

We all became extremely fit on the trip. We often walked two or three miles to see sights or get provisions and supplies. We swam almost every day, often for two or three hours or more. Most importantly, the constant motion of the boat meant that we were exercising constantly just to sit still. After a rough night at anchor, we sometimes woke with sore muscles from bracing to keep from moving in our bunks.

We drank lots of water. We kept the water in the holding tanks slightly chlorinated so that the tanks would not spoil.

We didn't see any illegal drugs on the trip, and only heard them mentioned once. We were at the WillyT, a floating bar in the British Virgin Islands. My key ring fell out of my pocket overboard, and the floating fob contained our money. I dove overboard to retrieve it, and when I returned a girl remarked "That must be good pot" if I went to that much trouble to get it back. I told her it was just my money. She seemed disappointed. Not a big story, but important because it was the only mention of drugs on the entire trip.

We were always aware of the dangers associated with living on the water and sailing in big weather. It scared us pretty badly a few times, but it never frightened us for long. In really rough weather or at night, we all wore inflatable life jackets and strapped in when sailing. In fairly rough weather, we all wore life jackets and usually strapped in. Only in the calmest sailing would we let the kids leave the cockpit without their life jackets, and then it was only to lie on the cabin roof. We were very aware of the stresses on the sails and rigging, and the kids didn't trim the sails in high winds.

The kids and I were poor swimmers before we left, but Nancy had gone to college on a swimming scholarship. Both Lena and Pender had swimming lessons the summer before we left, and once in the Caribbean they swam in wetsuits until their skills and confidence improved. The shorty wetsuits floated them just enough to keep them safe, and they also stayed in the water longer because they didn't get cold. By the second month of the trip, all of us were strong swimmers and skilled snorkelers.

Our dinghy was very fast and very powerful. We allowed the kids to use it by themselves, slowly increasing their freedom. For most of the trip, they needed to go slow, keeping the dinghy below planing speed. Gradually, they were allowed to go fast if an adult was in the boat, and by the end of the trip they could use their own judgment. They were invariably more cautious than I would have been. The kids almost always wore life jackets in the dinghy, and always did if there wasn't an adult in the boat.

While planning the trip, we spent a lot of time agonizing over whether we should carry a life raft on the boat. A really good life raft is extraordinarily expensive, and we knew that the average response time to an EPIRB (Emergency Position Indicating Radio Beacon) mayday call in the Caribbean is just a few hours. In an emergency our EPIRB would also broadcast our exact latitude and longitude, so we knew that a search and rescue team would find us very quickly. We rationalized that we could always use the dinghy as a life raft, since we always kept it fully inflated even if we stowed it on deck.

Luckily we discovered that we could buy a Zodiac Open Ocean life raft in French St. Martin for a little over $1800. At the time we rationalized that it would be stupid to risk our family just to save $1,800. If a decent raft had cost $3,000, we probably would have gone without. The Zodiac brand is considered a mid-quality raft, certainly not the best but much better than nothing. We stowed the life raft in one of *Mermaid*'s huge cockpit lockers along with the EPIRB and the Abandon Ship bag (containing safety equipment and ID) and hoped for the best.

Later experience towing the dinghy in open water through 50-knot wind gusts proved that carrying the life raft was the correct decision. In storm winds above 50 knots, even our heavy hard-bottom dinghy was more of a kite than a boat. There is no way to safely get an inflated dinghy from the foredeck to the water in high winds, and once in the water the dinghy will almost certainly blow away or capsize before you are able to climb aboard. It's important to remember that you will probably not be able to airfreight a packed life raft from the U.S. to any island. The bottles of compressed gas used to inflate the raft are considered hazardous freight.

We never observed or were directly involved with any crime. Until we got to Puerto Rico, we almost never saw a police officer. We rarely heard of crime of any sort except for occasional theft, which usually seemed to be cruisers stealing from cruisers. Puerto Rico, on the other hand, was full of heavily armed police and even more full of people needing to be policed. We rented a car and drove overland from Poncé to San Juan, then back. I have never seen so many drunk drivers.

The islands are remote and primitive. High-quality medical help might be days away if available at all, and we always assumed that we would have to fix whatever problems occurred. We spent lots of time treating small cuts and rashes, making sure that infection didn't set in. We paid lots of attention to ear care and didn't have any cases of swimmer's ear or ear infections.

Throughout the trip, we took the most basic precautions with our personal safety and never had any trouble. We locked our dinghy with a cable everywhere we went, we always locked our main hatches at night, and we closed up and locked the boat completely when we left her at anchor. Above all we tried to avoid putting ourselves in situations where "stupid" mistakes would put us in danger. We used the winches whenever possible to keep our fingers away from tight sail lines. We took our time.

From: Phil, Nancy, Lena and Pender
To: Mermaid Distribution
Email Sent: January 27, 2002

Hello, everybody!

This is our second Mermaid "Where are they?" contest. Our location is:

15 degrees, 51.6 minutes north

61 degrees, 36.1 minutes west

Bonus Question:

What is a Flying Gurnard?

To enter the contest, send a very short (less than 120 character) email to our Iridium page address.

The message format should be:

Where we are.

What is a Flying Gurnard?

Your name.

Your mailing address.

What type of postcard would you like: beach babe, beach stud, scenery, food.

The contest will close Monday at about 6 p.m., at which time we will send a standard, non-boring Mermaid report.

Good luck!

Phil, Nancy, Lena and Pender

From: Phil, Nancy, Lena and Pender
To: Mermaid Distribution
Email Sent: January 28, 2002

Hello, everyone:

Yeah, I know what you're thinking: These contests are all rigged. Nobody wins them unless they know the judges-well. There isn't any way for a normal, land-locked person to win these things. Well, you're right. However, there is something you should know, if you don't already. The answer to the second contest was exactly the same as the answer to the first contest, because we are back in "Les Saintes," Guadeloupe. We got only as far south as Martinique (we could see St. Lucia from where we were), and are now on our way back north.

The winner of our contest is an IT professional who is not a boater. He did, however, identify the hotel on the beach fronting our anchorage. The Internet is an amazing thing. We also got a winner whose name we don't recognize. Wow.

A flying gurnard, as all respondents got correctly, is a fish. It is an extremely cool fish about 18 inches long that hangs out over sandy bottoms "crawling" over the sand using its lower fins like legs. When threatened, it spreads its long pectoral fins (the ones on the side, right behind the gills). The spread fins make it look like a disk from above, with an electric blue trim around the perimeter of the disk. Unfortunately, when its fins are spread like this, it can only walk slowly on the bottom. If the threat continues, it must eventually retract his fins to swim off. They are very beautiful. Nancy and Pender saw two mating (spawning, probably) yesterday at the anchorage.

Flying Gurnard

We had been waiting on Martinique for about two weeks for the wind and seas to abate and give us a good passage. We finally got a little break and left on Saturday morning. We sailed 74 miles in about 10.5 hours for an average of 7 knots. That's pretty fast. The GPS logged a top speed of 11.1 knots, and we had times where we sailed over 8 knots for two hours or more. For the most part, the seas were a reasonable 6-8 feet tall, although lumpy. Toward the end of the trip, we were in 10 to 12-foot seas for about an hour. Those were a little on the big side. We were feeling pretty good about ourselves, then we met a family that did the same passage 12 hours later, leaving at 5 p.m. instead of 5 a.m. The wind blows about 5 knots faster at night, also. They had a wonderful passage, although their sails were very small (fully reefed) for most of the trip. The family has been cruising together for years, with three boys all 10 and under. They do all their passages longer than 5 hours at night, so the boys sleep through the whole thing. As the dad told me, "You never see the big waves coming anyway, so you might as well sail at night and let the kids sleep." Oddly enough, I can see the logic in that. Nancy and I (mostly Nancy) are not yet comfortable with the idea of not seeing ahead at night, although we are getting there. However, you can sail slower at night (with smaller sails), so the high winds of squalls and gusts will not affect you as much. On a long daylight passage, you have to keep your speed up so that you arrive at your destination with plenty of daylight to anchor.

For those of you who are experienced sailors, I know we are being wimpy. We're getting better, though. This passage was our first on a reach, although it was a close reach at times. All of our other passages have been upwind. Our next passage-Guadeloupe to Nevis, past Montessarat-should be a broad reach. We are looking forward to it.

Nancy has bought a plane ticket and will be flying to Miami 2/13 until 2/15 to attend the Miami boat show. We'll be in St. Maarten by then, so the kids and I will have an easy few days without her, catching up on school and projects. Company comes the next night, for a week, on the same flight, arriving at about 11 p.m. That means that I need to stay up past 9 p.m. two nights in a row. Doesn't seem possible.

Nancy and I went on a beautiful dive yesterday here at Pain de Sucre. Nothing special, but the huge schools of tiny colorful fish swimming through beautiful sponges and corals made the place magical.

We met two families with kids on the beach yesterday. One family is from Detroit, and the other from Redmond. The kids really like having other kids to play with. We'll probably stick around for an extra day or so and let them play.

That's all for now. I hope spring will spring soon at home.

Running Aground

We ran aground twice on this trip.

The first time was outside Fort de France in Guadeloupe. We had been chased out of les Saintes by incoming poor weather, and we were trying to anchor after a fairly difficult passage. We were north of the designated anchoring area motoring west into the setting sun at about four knots, picking out our anchoring spot. Nancy was on the bow, and I was steering. Both kids were on deck cleaning up and generally getting ready to anchor.

The boat slowed suddenly, not with a bang or a bump, but gently, as if we had run into a fishing net or perhaps a giant scoop of soft-serve ice cream. I looked down and saw that our digital depth sounder (with its transducer in the bow, immediately ahead of the keel) still showed 20 feet of water. Odd, I thought, it felt as if we ran aground. On the bow, Nancy could not see down through the sun glare on the water. I leaned over the starboard rail and could see a beautiful grassy bottom about two feet below the water surface. We were stuck in the mud to the back of the keel. In the cockpit the depth sounder now read 2 feet. "Thanks," I said. At least, that's what I think I said.

I was pretty sure that the propeller and water pickup were still clear of the mud, so I tried to back off. No movement. No movement whatsoever. We had towed the dinghy during the passage, so I jumped in and tried to tow the boat off with the dinghy while Nancy backed *Mermaid's* motor. Still no movement.

I ran the dinghy to *Mermaid's* bow - the dinghy propeller just grazed the mud bottom - and Pender helped me load the anchor and all 100 feet of chain into the dinghy. I then ran the anchor aft and slightly starboard of *Mermaid* and dropped it over the side of the dinghy. I climbed aboard the sailboat and we put Lena in the dinghy on the aft port quarter, pulling *Mermaid* off and upwind. Nancy backed the engine, and I used the anchor winch to pull *Mermaid* free. Sluuuuuurp.

So far, so good. But as the boat came free of the mud, Nancy turned the wheel and backed to starboard so that *Mermaid* wouldn't back over Lena. Taken by itself, this was a good decision. Unfortunately, I had continued to keep tension on the anchor chain as we backed, and the still tight chain hooked over the bulb on the base of the keel. Most sailboats are not particularly maneuverable when anchored by the keel, and *Mermaid* was no exception. After a slight discussion about how it would be a good idea to leave the engine in neutral, I grabbed a mask and fins and dove on the keel, dreading the mess I knew I would find. Luckily I was able to clear the chain in a couple of dives, and we were able to back into clear water and recover the anchor without further incident. There were plenty of people watching us as we made our way into the anchorage and found our place for the night, but none of them applauded. In a way, I was disappointed.

The only damage to the boat was some slight loss of bottom paint where the chain had rubbed on the starboard bow and the keel.

This all happened on Nancy's birthday. Instead of a nice quiet dinner and a pleasant evening in Les Saintes, incoming weather and misfortune meant that all she got for her birthday was a good story to tell later. We did make her a nice chocolate mousse.

The other time we ran aground was slightly more serious. We were sailing inshore on the south coast of Puerto Rico near La Paraguera. The water was brown and cloudy and we were not able to see the bottom as we sailed northeast looking for an anchorage south of the phosphorescent bay the guidebooks are so excited about. We were navigating strictly by pilotage, taking compass sightings of hills and landmarks to miss the several reefs and shoals in the area. In fact, we had just set the chart down after satisfying ourselves that we were clear of the hazards when we bumped and stumbled our way onto one of those reefs. A quick look over the side verified that we were on top of a fairly flat reef, although there were several taller coral heads to both port and starboard. We would float free, then bump down and lean slightly as the one-foot swell passed through.

After a short period of yelling and screaming while we stowed the sails, Nancy got into the dinghy and I handed her the lower end of the spinnaker halyard tied to about 80 feet of line. She did her best to pull the mast top over and into the wind and get us off the reef, but the dinghy wasn't strong enough to lean *Mermaid* very far, and there we sat.

I was starting to get very, very worried. The unusually high tide, caused by an unlikely alignment of the planets, was going out. We kept a Fortress FX-23 anchor in the cockpit, rigged to 30 feet of heavy chain and 200 feet of nylon rode. I had just gotten the collapsible anchor assembled when two very nice men arrived in their ancient wooden outboard-powered fishing boat. I noticed, but didn't seem to mind, the fluorescent green paint transferring from their hull to ours as we bumped in the chop. They did not speak English and they did not understand the little Spanish I thought I knew, but they took our anchor and set it as far from the boat as possible behind and slightly up-wind from us. I wound the nylon rode onto our jib sheet winch and cranked it tight, while Nancy and the fishermen applied pressure to the spinnaker halyard.

When a swell came through, *Mermaid* would float free and move three or four feet aft. I would tighten the rode, and on the next swell we would move again. We came off the reef fairly quickly, with almost no damage to the boat except that we knocked all the bottom paint and epoxy coating from the bottom of the iron keel. I looked up to see our fishermen friends right off the stern of the boat. They had retrieved our stern anchor as soon as the line went slack, keeping the line away from the propeller. Later Nancy told me that a freak wave had almost put their fishing boat into her dinghy while they both pulled full throttle on the halyard. I thanked them and asked them to hang around for a moment while we got everything straightened out, but they just smiled, waved, and drove away. We backed into clear water and got the anchor and lines aboard. I then grabbed $100 out of our stash, stuck it into the plastic ring on a six-pack of beer, and took off in the dinghy to chase down the two fishermen. They took my (cheap, warm) beer and cheerfully offered me one (good, cold) from their cooler, but when they saw the money they tried to get me to take it back. "No," I said, "it's yours. You saved me. Spend it on something fun."

"It's not necessary," they said.

"I know, but I don't want it back! Thanks again!" I said, and drove off.

"But I have a Viking 45," the man at the stern called after me.

I stuttered a little, then told him to spend it on gas. A Viking 45 is a 45-foot sport fishing battle wagon, made for Marlin fishing in the open ocean and worth three to five times what our sailboat was worth. I trust I didn't offend him.

St. Maarten Yacht Club. Bar on the right, grill on the left.

From: Phil, Nancy, Lena and Pender
To: Mermaid Distribution
Email Sent: February 17, 2002

Hello, everyone!

We've had a somewhat forceful request to send out another letter (Hi Mom), so I realized it's been some time since the last one. I hope you all still remember whom this is from.

Since the last letter we have traveled to Sint Maarten (thaat's Dutch for St. Martin, which is French for St. Martin). Sailing north from Martinique was great because we finally had winds behind us, at least for some of the journey. It's been a windy winter here, so we listened very carefully to the weather every morning trying to pick our "weather window" for each inter-island hop. Experienced cruisers don't pay a lot of attention to the weather reports and like to sail at night (reason: "You can't see the big waves in the dark"). Since anchoring in a strange port in the dark is a bad idea, and we like to sail during the day, we often have to sail fast to make the next island by dark. Sailing fast means that the big seas are even rougher on the boat, so it's more important for us to pick good weather. Luckily, this is a very fast boat. We often average over 7 knots anchor up to anchor down on a passage. Our top speed so far (according to the GPS) is an extraordinary 11.1 knots (which we've done twice). I believe that we hit that speed right before we hit the trough of the wave we had just fallen off.

Anyway, we are more comfortable sailors, and worry less about what to do when, etc. As often happens, once we became more comfortable, nature slapped us in the face. We had just sailed from Les Saintes to the southern tip of Guadeloupe, with Lena driving and doing great, when we got hit with our first williwaw right after rounding the southern tip of the island. Once we got in behind the land, the 15 to 20-knot tradewinds were "shadowed" by the island and we were not able to sail as fast as we wanted. On the passage, we had the sails "reefed," which means that they were smaller. Once we got in behind the island and the wind dropped, we let out all the sails to try to sail faster in the lighter winds. Everyone was in the cockpit, the sun was out, and everything was great. Then, literally out of nowhere, a wind gust of at least 40-50 knots came right off the mountains of the island. We leaned way over, putting the lee (downwind) rail of the boat at least six inches underwater. I grabbed the helm and turned into the wind until the gust passed, then we reduced sail, started the motor, and drove to the anchorage one or two miles up the coast.

We tried to visit Nevis again on our trip north, but once we anchored off Nevis, slept the night, and got up in the morning preparing to go ashore, we got a weather report that there were large northerly swells and 20 to 25-knot winds forecast for the next day. Since we were headed north that was not a good prospect, so we did not go ashore and instead spent the entire day motoring 60 miles to St. Maarten (the winds were too light to sail and make the 5:30 p.m. bridge into the sheltered lagoon). The more perceptive reader will already have guessed that the forecast conditions did not materialize for two days, so both missing Nevis and motoring the entire trip were unnecessary. Better safe than sorry, I suppose. We had to leave for two reasons: The north swell would have made the anchorage extremely uncomfortable, and we had to get Nancy to the St. Maarten airport to fly back to Miami for the boat show. She had a great time, and was able to see our sister-in-law Stacy one evening.

It is nice to be back in St. Maarten, which is where we started the trip. We have taken care of some minor mechanical problems and seen some old friends. We also made some great new friends on the trip north. We've met three or four boats with kids on them, all filled with nice people. It seems that once we turned north in Martinique we sort of entered the bulk of the cruisers flowing north for the season. We will leapfrog each other toward the Bahamas in the spring.

We are currently anchored in Great Bay, off Philipsburg. We are cleaning and re-arranging things in preparation for picking up our first guests, a couple and their daughter from Seattle. They will be here for a week. The wind is also picking up, so we don't know what we'll do for the week or how far we'll go.

We will stay in this area until the finish of the Heineken Cup on March 3. The Heineken Cup is a large sailboat race for, mostly, large sailboats. There are supposed to be 200-300 boats entered. We are all volunteering to help.

After the regatta, we will head to the BVI for a month or so. It looks like another couple will be joining us in early April in the American Virgin Islands.

The kids are taking sailing lessons while we are here in St. Maarten. They sail on Optimist dinghies in the harbor. Pretty cool, although they think it's pretty normal.

We hope you all have a great Valentine's Day!

Phil, Nancy, Lena and Pender

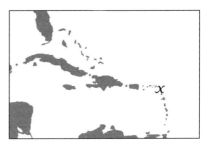

From: Phil, Nancy, Lena and Pender
To: Mermaid Distribution
Email Sent: March 4, 2002

Hello everyone!

We wish that we were sending this message from the BVI, but an extremely strange and odd weather system has set up in the tropical Atlantic, so we will wait here in St. Maarten for one more week. A "tropical wave" is generating 20-foot seas in open water. Tropical waves are normally summer weather systems that originate near Africa and can cause hurricanes in the Caribbean. However, the water temperature here is much too low to support any kind of hurricane, so wind and waves are all we'll get from this system. Since our boat is only 40 feet long, we think we'll stay here for a while.

The St. Maarten Yacht Club Heineken Regatta just ended yesterday. It was amazing. More than 220 boats of all sizes (22 to more than 100 feet long) came to race in a series of 4 races over three days. Nancy and Lena sold T-shirts and worked on one of the start boats. Pender and I drove the "rover" boat-ferrying people around, running for beer, and helping with one minor medical incident (turned out to be a sprained, not dislocated or broken, elbow). Lena also helped me on the last day when they didn't need her on a committee boat. Probably half of the racing boats were groups of people who chartered yachts and then raced them. Some of the chartered yachts were identical to ours, many were slightly larger. Many of these charter groups brought full sets of racing sails to use on their rented boats. We saw a few boat crashes, but nowhere near as many as I thought we would see, and as far as I know the hurt elbow was the only injury that required medical attention.

There were parties every night of the regatta. Each party had one or two live bands, drink stands, custom-rolled-cigar stands, and T-shirt sales stands. Pender and Lena went to one party and made it until about 9 p.m. Nancy and I rested up and managed to stay out until about 11 p.m. on another night. We were very proud of ourselves. We were told that the really interesting stuff at the parties starts at about 3 a.m. It would have to be pretty interesting to be worth 3 a.m. The kids did, however, get to see Roy Disney, Walt's son. Roy was here sailing his yacht Pyewacket, which is an extremely tall, narrow, and long sailboat that sailed approximately twice as fast as any other boat here. Lena and Pender were also able to go aboard Pyewacket after the racing was over and have a look around. Very nice of the Pyewacket crew since the boat is not normally open to the public.

The boat that we used during the regatta was a 13 foot Boston Whaler, with a 35 HP motor. It ran great (the motor was brand new) and we covered a lot of ground. It's pretty cool to be five miles offshore in a 13-foot boat.

Our first guests were here right before the regatta. Their visit went well, and we saw a lot of the island even though we lost two days to weather. On those two days, instead of traveling by boat, we got in a bus and visited the butterfly farm here on the island. We arrived in the morning and were able to see them emerge from their chrysalises. You can go to the farm's website and learn what plants to plant in your area to attract native butterfly species. Each butterfly has a specific plant that they need to lay their eggs on, and then various plants can provide nectar for the adult butterflies to eat. The web site is www.thebutterflyfarm.com.

After visiting the butterfly farm, we went to a great wading beach, where it was shallow for a long way out. The kids (Lena and Pender and our guests' 14 year old daughter) got bored with wading, so we walked to another beach called Orient Beach to body surf and see the sights. To get to Orient Beach, we walked though an area called Club Orient. This is a world class nudist resort. I'm sure that you have many, many questions for me regarding the resort, but I will answer five of them:

1. It was not as weird as you might imagine.
2. Yes, they were playing volleyball. Not Olympic class, but there were a few long volleys.
3. The kids have never walked faster on a beach in their lives.
4. The women, as a group, seemed to be fairly attractive with at least fair muscle tone. Perhaps the less fit women elected not to go nude.
5. The men did not seem to feel any such social pressure to maintain their level of physical fitness.

Orient Beach was great. We had some pizza and ribs, went body surfing in six-foot surf, and went back to the boat in a taxi. It may have been the most expensive day of the trip, but it was fun.

Our guests brought us five dozen corn tortillas. We have been eating enchiladas and corn tortilla quesadillas since. Very nice. They also brought us some homemade cookies, which were great. The cookies made us realize how much we miss baked goods, so I fixed the oven so we could bake. Now we make cookies ourselves.

We continue to meet new friends on the trip. There are not a lot of families cruising with their kids, but those that are almost always share many of our core values and concerns. We have met very few cruising kids without self-discipline and self-control. In fact, just now Lena and Pender took the dinghy over to another boat to get two other kids and go to the beach. The four of them went to the beach, then they were able to see a squall approach and they made it back to our friends' boat before most of the wind and rain started. We assume that, once we get back, life will be difficult for Lena until she gets her driver's license. She feels pretty free now, being able to get around by dinghy.

From here we hope to get to the BVI Thursday or Friday, then hang around there and the USVI for a while, then meet some friends in Puerto Rico. Although things beyond that are extremely vague, we will probably end up in Ft. Lauderdale the first week in June and truck the boat home. Our last plan, sailing across the Gulf of Mexico to Houston, looks to be a difficult and dangerous trip. We are trying to avoid difficult and dangerous things.

That's about all for now. We're trying to get a picture or two to send. The next email will probably be only pictures.

Hope you are all having a great spring.

Phil, Nancy, Lena and Pender Rink

SMYCHR

The Saint Maarten Yacht Club Heineken Regatta is a big three-day sailboat race on the first weekend in March (or so), involving more than 200 big sailboats. On the first day they race from the Dutch side to the French side. Then everyone anchors in Marigot Harbor and there is a big party. On day two, they race from the French side to the Dutch side. Everyone anchors in Simpson Bay and there is a big party. On day three, to be completely different, they race all the way around the island before the big party. I think there were some other parties, too. Despite all that, the event is actually about sailboat racing! People came from all over the world to race here. Some of them have beautiful specially built racing sailboats and professional racing crews that fly in especially for the event. Most of them are part-time sailors who charter yachts for the weekend. Some of the charter competitors bring their own racing sails and rigging. Some local cruisers also raced.

We were not experienced sailors, we didn't want to break our house, and we had no idea what the racing rules were. We thought the best way to see the races would be to volunteer. We were already members of the host St. Maarten Yacht Club (SMYC) so we signed up and hung around the volunteer meetings and got great assignments that came with front row seats to the races. Jerry Blakeslee, the St. Maarten yacht broker who sold us our boat, is also a lifetime SMYC commodore. It was his Boston Whaler I drove as a "rover" boat, ferrying race officials, supplies, beer and other essentials to the committee boats before and during the races. I also towed in a dismasted boat and ferried an injured sailor to shore. Nancy and Lena worked on one of the committee boats, operating the flags and air horns to coordinate the starts. Pender helped either Nancy or me.

We all had a great time because we weren't spectators. Being involved made the whole thing much more interesting. From the start boat they saw most of the boats going top speed, in very close quarters, from right up close. They saw one or two small collisions, lots of near misses, crazy sailing, and some very fast boats. They also met some very nice people who managed and directed the races. The races are run by an international team and are extremely well managed. We also met international members of the Yachting Press, and the kids were wide-eyed over their tour of one of the professional racing boats.

It was really amazing to see Marigot Harbor, on the French side of the island, completely packed with racers anchored not more than 30 feet apart with a two-foot chop blasting through the anchorage. Their anchor lights made the harbor look like an old-fashioned Christmas tree. The next morning was something of a madhouse when boats raised their anchors in shifts to get ready for their final race to Phillipsburg. At least one captain tried to sail off his anchor in the crowded harbor. He ended up drifting into a huge megayacht before getting his boat under control.

The parties were all huge events with live bands, cigar rollers, happy sunburned sailors, and Heineken beer in skinny little cans.

There are sailing races up and down the island chain. Antigua Yacht Week is a little later in the year or we would have gone to that, too. As it was, we left St. Maarten as soon as we could after the Regatta, to head west.

From: Phil, Nancy, Lena and Pender
To: Mermaid Distribution
Email Sent: March 9, 2002

Hello from *Mermaid.*

We made it to the Virgin Islands. The trip from St. Maarten to the British Virgin Islands (BVI) is through 80 nautical miles (about 90 dirt miles) of open ocean called the Anegada passage. The Anegada passage is known for being rough, with big waves, so we were very careful about picking our time to cross. As it turned out, we left one or two days earlier than most of the boats waiting in St. Maarten, but had a great crossing. The waves were 6-8 feet tall, with occasional waves of 12 feet or higher, and winds of 15-20 knots. We left at 3 a.m., planning on a 3:30 p.m. arrival, which we hit on the nose with an average speed of 7.1 knots. We had all the sails up for almost the entire crossing. Except for a light rain shower at 6 a.m., we didn't get wet. Very little spray and no waves came aboard.

All in all, it was our nicest crossing of the trip so far. Going downwind is way easier than going upwind. On this crossing, we were on a broad reach for most of the trip. This means that both the wind and in this case the waves were from behind us on the starboard (right) corner of the boat. We had to head slightly higher (more upwind) than we wanted to keep the jib (forward sail) full of wind, but it all worked out great at the end.

As we neared Virgin Gorda at the end of the trip, Nancy yelled, "Turn left!" I did, and we narrowly missed what we think was a humpback whale and her calf. In any case there were two of them, both with split blowholes (like an upturned nostril set flush into their backs). They swam parallel to us for a few minutes, and we think we saw another pair farther off. These whales were huge-at least as big as the boat, probably bigger.

Here in the BVI, we've been to the Baths (which were beautiful but crowded), and to the Bitter End resort. It is high season and most of the anchorages are fairly crowded. It's also our first spot where most of the cruisers are American. Those Americans sure talk a lot. They don't say much, though. I wonder if the French did the same thing but since we don't speak French we didn't notice. We are now in Great Harbor on Jost Van Dyke, waiting to go ashore for the "FOXY's Music Festival." How cool is that?

We had an unusual occurrence today, so we decided to take a picture to remember it. The attached picture is of the crew of *Mermaid*. The careful observer will notice that we are sailing downwind-wing and wing. That's right, with the wind. At about eight knots. Warm, calm, standing upright downwind. We had heard that it was nice and it was! Wow. We hope to go downwind again in April. In case you are wondering, we have an autopilot to steer the boat. I'm sorry I'm not wearing a shirt. I'll try to dress better next time.

That's all for now. We hope your spring is going well.

Phil, Nancy, Lena and Pender

Wing and wing in the BVI.

Business

Nancy and I did not have any day-to-day work responsibilities, but we did need to stay in touch with business contacts in the states. We found that our communication systems were more than adequate. In addition, if needed, we could easily have gotten back home with less than a week's notice.

If we had needed to stay in closer contact, the trip would not have been worthwhile. There were many places and circumstances where communication was difficult or impossible. A fixed communication schedule would mean that you would be forced to travel despite the weather conditions, or forced to stay in more populated or congested areas.

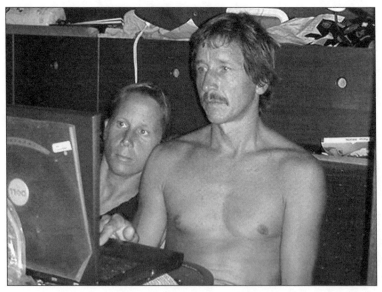

Nancy and I hard at work.

From: Phil, Nancy, Lena and Pender
To: Mermaid Distribution
Email Sent: March 22, 2002

Hello, everyone:

Announcing the third "Where are they" contest for *Mermaid.* Our latitude is 64 degrees, 43.32 minutes W, our longitude is 18 degrees, 18.87 minutes N. The extra credit bonus question is: "What is the Tektite project, and why do we care?" Email entries to: 8816XXXXXXXX@msg.iridium.com, 120 characters max. Be sure to include your name and address. Prizes will be what they are.

We will be at a good email source Sunday and Monday. Please feel free to send whatever pictures, etc., you want to send (to our hotmail address). We'd love to see them.

We have spent the last week at the same place, without moving, on a free, government-installed mooring (like a permanent anchor). This seems odd, but it is good to recover after the hustle-bustle of St. Maarten and the BVI. Pender and Lena have spent a lot of time jumping into the water, using a fender hung from the spinnaker pole as a rope swing.

We have friends coming to meet us in Puerto Rico the first week in April. Soon we will mosey over to meet them. It seems odd not to have to worry too much about the winds and weather. In fact, we had a strong rain and windstorm last night. It was refreshing, and washed the salt off the boat. It wasn't scary, we didn't worry about the anchor, and it's doesn't affect our plans in the least.

Today we hauled out the spinnaker and ran it up the mast to see what it looks like and if we can use it on the trip to the Bahamas. It looks good, and we will probably practice with it in the coming weeks. If you don't know, a spinnaker is the huge, colorful sail used to go downwind faster than you can using the mainsail and jib. The spinnaker for our boat is about 40' tall and about 25-30' across at the bottom. It is red, white and blue. If you screw up flying a spinnaker, you can make a great big mess in a hurry. I can't wait to try it.

We are making plans about our trip to the Bahamas. We will leave Boqueron on the west coast of Puerto Rico approximately April 14 and arrive somewhere in the Bahamas between two days and two weeks later, depending on whether we go straight or hop down the north coast of the Dominican

Republic. We will then dink around in the Bahamas until we get too scared of the hurricane season. If anyone is interested, we are looking for experienced crew for the trip. Crew should be able to stand watch alone, be available for uncertain amounts of time, and be less grumpy than I am. We will pay travel and food expense, and provide some sort of sleeping place. Please email us if you are interested.

In the BVI, Nancy and I were able to go diving twice on the wreck of the Rhone. The Rhone was a lowly mail ship, but the wreck of the Rhone is one of the most famous dive spots in the world. The wreck was featured in the movie "The Deep," and the water there is clearer than Jacqueline Bisset's T-shirt. We also went snorkeling at Anegada, which was beautiful, and we saw a spotted eagle ray jump four feet out of the water twice while we were sailing down to the Baths. We also spent about three hours at the Baths, which is a beautiful boulder/beach combination where you can wander around in tidal grottoes. Normally, the Baths are extremely crowded with charter boats and busloads of cruise ship passengers, but we were there at the end of the day and there wasn't anybody around. The kids found all kinds of abandoned clothing and accessories and brought me a new pair of Tommy Bahama shoes. Too bad I'm never going to wear shoes again.

That's all for now. We'll try to send a picture or two soon when we find a shore station.

Phil, Nancy, Lena and Pender

Staying in Touch

One of the biggest mistakes we made on the trip was to under-estimate our communications capability and our desire for contact with our friends from home. Setting up the trip we discouraged, or at least didn't encourage, emails from home because we didn't think we would be able to retrieve it all. While we did have some problems downloading email, we couldn't get enough news from home and were always glad to hear from friends.

For boat-to-boat communication we had a built-in VHF radio installed in the cabin and a hand-held VHF we kept in the cockpit. The Standard Horizon Submersible hand-held we used is an amazing radio. It got soaked, dropped, rained on, smashed, kicked, stepped on and treated with total disrespect. It still works extremely well, and it often picked up signals better than the built-in radio with its mast-top antenna. The cruising community used VHF radio for morning radio nets in St. Maarten, Antigua, and Georgetown. We used the hand-held VHF radio to stay in touch with the boat when part of the family went ashore.

We used FRS (Family Radio Service) radios to stay in touch with each other when the whole family went ashore. We bought rechargeable NiMH batteries for these radios before we left home. Batteries are not easy to buy down-island.

For email and safety communication we brought an Iridium satellite phone. Voice communication over the Iridium phone was spectacular and expensive. The Iridium system uses several dedicated satellites in low polar orbits to maintain constant, reliable contact with the entire surface of the globe. The phone is the size of an early cell phone and the service is great. The connection was always much clearer than VHF or SSB radios, and for a one-year trip the cost of the equipment and service was much less than an installed SSB radio, antenna and tuner. We even used the phone to call family on Christmas. In an emergency the portable and reliable satellite phone system would be much more useful than the radios, although the hand-held VHF radio would be required for close-in communication with the potential rescuers. Internet over the Iridium phone was reliable and fairly convenient, but it was slow (9800 baud) and much more expensive ($1.50 per minute) than at home. We could download a Wind and Waves chart from NOAA or check email in just a few minutes. When we needed to, we could transfer huge files, even at sea.

Email over Pocketmail (a landline system using a dedicated hand-held unit), HAM or SSB would not have been satisfactory for our use because the file size is limited and there is no Internet access. Unlike email over SSB, email using the Iridium system is perfectly legal for obtaining quotes and conducting business. Globalstar, another satellite-based communication system that uses cell phones for part of the transmission path, did not cover the Caribbean during our trip.

We used a Hotmail email account. Hotmail accounts can be checked from any Internet café or other Internet connection, and can also be checked using Outlook Express over the Iridium line very quickly without having to go through a graphics-heavy (and therefore slow) web page. We begged everyone to be very careful using the address and to never send us automated greeting cards or otherwise misuse the address so we had very little "spam". We learned how to set up Outlook Express on our computer so we could see the size of the file before trying to download huge files. Hotmail does have a limit on the total size of all your email files, and our account was "frozen" a few times until we could get to an Internet café and clean things out.

Internet cafés in the Caribbean were spotty. On some islands they were plentiful and cheap, on others they were incredibly expensive. We usually found it more convenient to use the Iridium phone for email, and used cafes only when they were easy to find and we wanted to look around on the Internet. We were able to use cafés to do research for the kids' school reports.

We were amazed and disappointed at the varied quality of the telephone systems throughout the islands. For instance, there is no universal cell phone system, and it's virtually impossible and certainly wildly expensive to use one cell phone on every island. The landlines can be good or bad, and some phones on some islands would not work with pocket mail or other modem systems. On many islands you could not use calling cards from the United States or dial U.S. "1-800" numbers. When we arrived on St. Maarten you had to travel to Phillipsburg to use a calling card. Otherwise calls to the US were over $2 per minute. In the Bahamas the phones are a joke. Actually, BATELCO (BAhamas TElephone COmpany) phones are the basis for several jokes, none of which are funny. I tried to use an Internet station in Georgetown and was disconnected five times in 30 minutes. The sign above the monitor said, "This is the Bahamas, and the phones don't work very well. You pay the same whether the phones work or not."

In St. Maarten one business fronting the lagoon installed a compatible phone and sold phone cards for seven cents per minute to the states. Although we often had to wait in line for 30 minutes or more, it was a great chance for the kids to call their friends at home and us to straighten out some bill payment issues. Normal phone service from the islands to the states was approximately as expensive as the Iridium phone-$1.50 per minute.

One benefit of the Iridium service is a paging feature, where people can send you a short message of 120 characters or less for free. We loved to hear from people this way, even if their name or part of the message was dropped occasionally. The "message" chime would go off, often in the middle of the night, and everyone would wake up and rush to read the page. Some of our friends spent considerable time translating into license plate language and could send a lot of information. UcnSayLotsWOmnyLttrs. Since we checked email only once a week or so, we had people page us if they sent an urgent email. The page would tell us to check our email ASAP.

Email was very useful for boat-to-boat communication, helping us stay in touch with our new cruising friends so that we could meet further along our voyage.

Before we left we printed boat cards, like business cards, and laminated them to make them water-resistant. The cards had our boat name, our names, our email and Iridium numbers, and our P.O. Box number in the states. We gave them out to visitors and friends.

The kids really missed hearing from their friends on the trip. None of their friends used email before we left, and few tried to stay in touch. We all really appreciated hearing from those who did.

We wanted to share our trip with friends from home, and we hoped that we would have visitors. From our previous boating experience, we knew that the best boat guests were the people who really wanted to be there. At home, we almost always split boating expenses and rarely try to talk anyone into going boating with us. We knew on this trip that visits would be logistically difficult and that any visitors would have to be extremely flexible. We also knew that the boat would be crowded during a visit and everyone would have to keep expectations down for a visit to be successful. We invited anyone who wanted to come, then tried to paint a fairly realistic, if bleak, picture of what they could expect. Only two families came down to visit us, but their terrific attitudes and flexibility meant that both visits went really well even though both occurred during poor weather.

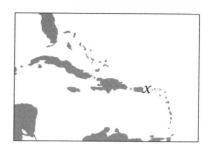

From: Phil, Nancy, Lena and Pender
To: Mermaid Distribution
Email Sent: March 25, 2002

Just the picture.

The Flying Mermaid Family

From: Phil, Nancy, Lena and Pender
To: Mermaid Distribution
Email Sent: April 1, 2002

Hello, all:

Well, spring is the seasonof change and growth, and this month has been no exception for our family.

During a rather heated argument over algebra homework last week, Lena was excused from the rest of the trip. She feels that it is time for her to try her luck on her own, and her mother and I are inclined to agree. She can be reached at the "Bag of Blues Beach Bar and Bandstand" (BB B BB), Green Cay, BVI. she will be cleaning floors in the morning and tending bar at night. We wish her well. She took her saxophone, so she's always got her music to fall back on.

Pender was not interested in being the only child on the boat, so new he is working at the Navy range on Vieques as a "spotter." He runs out with a golf flag after each bombing run and marks which crater was made by which plane. We are extremely proud of him. He feels that his quick reflexes, good eyesight, and small profile will really help him in his new job. He will also have plenty of time to work on his tan, and between training days he plans to learn to fly one of the big jets. We are so proud of him. The commanding general said within 10 years Pender will either be a top gun or a top target. Apparently there are lots of openings for advancement. You can reach Pender at: Youth Outreach, Puerto Rico; Department of the Navy, Washington, DC. Please allow eight weeks for communication (more if the range is hot, because then the mail planes won't go anywhere near the island).

Nancy and I traded the sailboat and our house in Washington for the boat you see in the attached picture. It is an "Air Cushion Transport" designed to run fast in rough, shallow seas. It is soon to be retired from the Norwegian navy, and has already been painted to resemble a small island. The deal was tough to negotiate, but then the captain of the ship somehow got the idea that the deed on our Washington property

included mineral rights, and Camano Island was located very near the vast oil reserves in the ANWR. Suddenly, the deal was completed. We are having some trouble getting the final title on the ship, but we assume that will all clear up when Captain "Slick" Willy Gunderson gets back to Oslo.

We will be running the classic northwestern Caribbean triangle route, carrying wrecked cars and steel boat hulls from the Bahamas to the Dominican Republic, then "pre-Castro" grade cigar wrappers and baseballs to Cuba, then Chinese trans-shipped inexpensive polyester pareos and loud shirts to the Bahamas for the cruise ship trade. We call our ship "Fast Noisy Island" and will be able to make two full runs before we need to refill the fuel tanks. The twin turbine engines probably use a lot of fuel-we'll have to see. By the way, does anyone know where we can get "Jet A" in a marina? We will also have T-shirts printed to help us ease through customs, if you know what I mean (and I think some of you know what I mean).

We hope that you all have a great April. We know we will be busy for a while, getting the new business started, but we will try to keep you updated. At times in the future our communications may be monitored, so we want to establish a code: If you get a message that says: "There is a party in Samana," that means get to Samana as soon as possible bringing lawyers, guns and money. Don't worry, Mom. Everything will be fine.

All our love:

Phil, Nancy, Lena and Pender

Actually, just Phil and Nancy.

From: Phil, Nancy, Lena and Pender
To: Mermaid Distribution
Email Sent: April 2, 2002

Howdy:

So, here is what we are really doing.

We just got into Puerto Rico yesterday. We meet guests in Fajardo on the east coast of PR on Saturday night. A week from Saturday, or soon after, we will leave for the Bahamas.

The USVI and Puerto Rico have been everything we dreaded about returning to the U.S. Vauge and bizarre customs minefields, inoperative phones, and loud stereos in the anchorages. Oddly, the area is also the most beautiful that we've seen. The coral is the healthiest of anywhere we've been, we've seen lots of turtles, and the sand on the beaches is fine and white. We are still extremly vague about when and how we will return to civilization.

We have left the land of easy Internet. Please don't send any more pictures. We do love to get Iridium pages and standard test messages up to about 10K (on or two pages) to our Hotmail account. Please send those. The kids would especially like to hear from their friends.

If anyone has saved all of these messages from Mermaid, please continue saving them. We have not been able to keep a copy of each and would like to get copies of all of them when we get back. Thanks.

I'll keep it short. Take care of yourselves.

Adios:

Phil, Nancy, Lena and Pender

How to Have Fun

We have always been a fairly serious family. We do lots of things together, but we argue better than we laugh. The kids have always worked in our family business, and the are very good business people, but we wanted to do something new on this trip. We wanted to just play. The trip was work enough-just finding a safe place to anchor or a safe time to make a passage could be serious, hard work. Whenever we found something that looked like fun, we tried to do it, and when we had to do serious things, we tried to make them fun, too.

At home on Puget Sound, we don't do a lot of swimming. Fifty-five-degree water is not fun. Sometimes, when the water is shallow and calm, it warms up to about 65 or 70 and we can swim for a few minutes before we start to shiver uncontrollably. Our home waters are also murky, with 15-foot visibility common and 30-foot visibilty exceptional.

The crystal-clear warm water in the tropics was a gift straight from God to our family, and we couldn't get enough of it. We were rarely anchored in a new spot for more than a half-hour before someone was snorkeling around the boat. As long as the kids wore wet suits we were not concerned about them. They understood and used the buddy system and soon knew the names of more reef fish than Nancy or I. We had several plastic cards in the cockpit with color pictures of all the fish, and three or four guidebooks in the cabins. They would study these until they could identify almost every fish we saw by name, sex, and age. They didn't require much encouragement to try swimming further and diving deeper, and often swam all the way into the beach.

We all got more or less comfortable with the big fish we saw snorkeling, although there were exceptions. Lena got pretty freaked out by a six-foot nurse shark that exploded from the sand 10 feet below us at Anegada. Pender and I got a little nervous about a five-foot barracuda in the Bahamas that seemed a little more agressive than normal. However, Pender was also the bravest on the boat. He was absolutely not intimidated by the six-foot lemon sharks swimming under the boat at Waderick Wells in the Bahamas, and snorkeled fearlessly when they were around.

Nancy and I are experienced scuba divers. We took most of our equipment and bought tanks and lead weights down-island. We made about twelve dives apiece during the trip. The dives we made were great and beautiful, and we saw some amazing things like hammerhead sharks and turtles, but if we had only snorkeled during the trip neither of us would have been disappointed.

We also had an inflatable kayak on board that belonged completely to the kids. They would take the kayak and explore on their own, leaving the dinghy for Nancy and me. We would keep a pretty good eye on them while they used the kayak, however, so that they weren't run over by a dinghy in the harbor or the trade winds wouldn't blow them out to sea if they lost a paddle.

There were beaches in most harbors. We figured out what they were for fairly early in the trip. We didn't carry a lot of buckets and shovels, but the kids managed to build incredible sand castles anyway. We learned that towels do not belong on the beach. We used Pareos to lie on the sand. They sook out quickly and were much easier to wash than towels. In fact, we didn't use towels after swimming either, but but we dried off with synthetic chamois ("the absorber"). The chamois were easy to wring our and dried better than towels. We kept our towels down in the cabin and tried not to get them wet.

We did some sightseeing and tourist stuff but were careful to not make it a burden. Forts and cities were more adventure than fun.

We downplayed the holidays, and didn't have any packages shipped to or from home. We had a small celebration on the boat in Nonsuch Bay in Antigua, and invited a young French couple for Christmas Eve dinner. They were both schoolteachers in French Guyana, and we had a wonderful evening.

We rarely play board games at home. On the boat we played a game (usually "Upwords") three or four times a week, right before bedtime. It was quiet, it was dark outside, and we weren't tired of each other's company. This may be the part of the trip I miss the most.

Very occasionally we would rent a DVD and watch it on our laptop computer. We did this rarely enough that it was a real treat. We would also occasionally visit other boats for a "movie night", since many boats had VCRs and movie collections. Often the kids would go to the other boat to watch their movie and the parents would come to ours to sit and talk.

On their own the kids started making animated "Lego" movies. They would use the digital still camera to take a series of pictures of the little Lego figures doing something, then string the pictures together using the computer to make a short movie.

We embraced the time we spent doing nothing, and never considered that time wasted. We all read voraciously. We dozed on the beach. We hung out on the deck. We floated in the dinghy. We sang songs with each other and alone. Lena and Pender played music, with Lena on her flute or saxophone and Pender on his harmonica. We discussed philosophy, religion, engineering, politics, sociology, esthetics, biology, and technology. Nancy and I really wanted the kids to have goofy fun with us, to do things that aren't a part of their routine. They went skinny dipping and lay naked in the sun with us (well, sometimes), they drove the boat, they drove the dinghy, they tended bar, and they went shopping. Because we usually had the time and the situations were relatively simple, we tried to let them make as many decisions as possible.

We met up with our friends from *TIME* in the British Virgin Islands, and we went scuba diving together. Their children had learned to dive and were certified in Trinidad during the previous summer. We met at Jost Van Dyck for the FOXY's Music Fest. FOXY's is a world-famous beach bar that defines "relaxed." After a quick basketball game at the island school, we were lying around the beach in hammocks having the children bring beers to us. Nancy mentioned that she and I wanted to go to the "WillyT", a famous floating bar in a cove on one of the southern islands. "Oh, no," Abby said. "You don't want to do that. We were there last week and that is no place to take the children."

"We don't want to take the children," Nancy said. "We heard that if you jump off the bar naked you get a T-shirt, and I want a shirt."

"Well, that sounds like fun," Abby answered. A few nights later, while the kids watched videos in their boat, Nancy and Abby got their T-shirts. They don't give shirts to men, or Robert and I would each have two. The kids later told us that they tried to watch us with binoculars, but we were too far away.

Time and Mermaid at the WillyT.

104 in ˙

From: Phil, Nancy, Lena and Pender
To: Mermaid Distribution
Email Sent: April 19, 2002

Hello, all:

We left Boqueron on the southwest coast of Puerto Rico yesterday morning at 5:30, about one hour before sunup. The water was glassy smooth in the harbor as we motored out through the cuts in the reef and into the Mona Passage between Puerto Rico and the Dominican Republic. We set sail and sailed straight through until 4:30 this morning, when the wind finally fell below 10 knots. We are now motoring through a large area north of the Dominican Republic that is notorious for "light and fluky winds" when there is a stalled trough in the area, which there is.

Last night was the first night that we have spent at sea, and it went very well. We watched thunderstorms drift southwest off Puerto Rico until early this morning, lighting up the skies behind us. We saw very few ships (three or four), and all of them were over the horizon. There are very few lights on the north coast of the DR, but there was a sliver of a moon and the skies were fairly clear until 3 a.m. or so, and the night was beautiful.

You have probably read about phosphorescence in seawater, where some of the plankton gives off light when disturbed. We have seen it often in Puget Sound, and it is spectacular. What I've never heard about, and we saw last night, was that the water is so clear here that you can see the wake of the keel and rudder glow with green fireflies six feet below the surface, leaving a vertical blue-green line glowing 20 feet or more behind the boat.

Over the last week, the crew of Mermaid has killed twice. Today, we hope to kill again. Tuesday, we found a conch (pronounced konk) large enough to clean, and ate conch savichi, which is raw conch soaked in lime juice with some cilantro. It didn't taste very good, but we'll try again soon in the Bahamas. In case you don't know, a conch is a snail about 12" long or bigger. Yesterday, Nancy caught our second fish of the trip, a cero, which is like a mackerel. We will eat it when we arrive somewhere.

And where are we going? Well, the Bahamas, eventually, but hopefully tomorrow night we will stay at West Caicos Island for a good night's sleep before continuing west. For those of you without the appropriate charts, that's 450 nautical miles, about the same as Denver to Albuquerque. Any 1962 Plymouth Valiant with the "drive" button pushed in could do that trip about 7 1/2 hours. We will do it in about 60-70 hours, assuming the wind comes back up this afternoon. Of course, we have a bigger trunk than the Valiant. By the way, because the winds are light the seas are also very small, only about 4-6 feet with a one-foot wind chop on top. Very smooth.

We were going to have a guest letter, written by our guests from last week. We'll send that out when it comes to us.

Adios,

Phil, Nancy, Lena and Pender Rink

From: Phil, Nancy, Lena and Pender
To: Mermaid Distribution
Email Sent: April 20, 2002

Hello, all:

We completed our long passage from Puerto Rico to the Turks and Caicos. We are currently sort of anchored at French Cay at the south tip of the Caicos Bank. I say sort of anchored because the bottom is hard coral, and there is nothing for the anchor to dig into. It hooks onto cracks and rocks in the bottom, so we won't drift far. The next anchorage is four hours further, and the thunderstorms have started again, so this will do for tonight.

Nancy and I really couldn't care less if we drag anchor a little. We've both had about six hours sleep in the last three days, and we spent yesterday and all last night dodging thunderstorms ("Which way is that one moving? I don't know-what about this one over here? That one's only three miles away-which way is it moving? Do you see any glowing in the rigging?"). Tonight we will sleep, and we'll start caring about stuff again tomorrow. The last half of the passage has been very difficult because of the thunderstorms and because there is very little wind. We have motored or motor-sailed two thirds of the way.

On the good-news side, we caught a five-pound skipjack tuna yesterday, and we just finished a very nice barbecued steak dinner. For those of you who haven't had it before, tuna can be cooked just like steak, medium rare, and it tastes really good.

The remainder of this letter is from our guests from two weeks ago. When they came down there were high winds and 13-foot seas that kept us away from the Spanish Virgins, but we ran for the south coast of Puerto Rico and had a great time anyway.

Be well.

Phil, Nancy, Lena and Pender

We are the Herringtons and were commissioned to write the latest Mermaid Report since we spent last week on the boat with the Rinks. First of all, they are great hosts. They even gave up the "master suite" for us and moved in to Pender's room. Pender got relegated to the couch in the "living room."

My wife and I and our 12-year-old daughter met the Rinks at Puerto Del Rey Marina on the east coast of Puerto Rico after flying in to San Juan from Albuquerque on Saturday night. The first night was in the relative "luxury" of a marina berth. We set sail the following morning and promptly sighted a U.S. Navy Boomer sub. Shortly thereafter the Coast Guard and a local coastal police boat intercepted us to maintain 1,000-yard clearance. A few years ago in Puget Sound, again on the Rinks' motor boat, we got within 100 yards of a Boomer. 9/11 sure has changed things.

We then proceeded to Puerto Patillas and saw flying eagle rays and porpoises. While there, we went snorkeling with a manatee. This was no Florida manatee. A clean specimen with no prop marks. Apparently this area is well known for manatees. Spent the night in that bay and then on to anchorage in the bay at Salinas. This is a heavy mangrove area. Mangroves are trees that live in seawater. Pender, our trusty dinghy captain, led the expedition into the mangroves with pelicans in the trees.

We then sailed on to Caja de Muertos, an island about 7 miles south of Ponce, PR. Nice island with a lighthouse and very nice government-developed camping area that is manned by 3-4 park rangers year-around. We spent two days there playing on the white sand beaches and crystal clear water, snorkeling, and climbing the hill to the lighthouse. The Spanish built the lighthouse in 1887-now with automated equipment compliments of the U.S. Coast Guard. The climb to the lighthouse was very interesting. Empty conch (Phil will remind me that this is pronounced "konk") shells which are a local delicacy (more later on this). Iguanas on the trail, sinkholes in the hillside, large termite nests in the trees, and interesting trees. The "tourist tree" is named for the flaky red bark that reminds the locals of sunburned tourists with flaky skin (I wasn't that bad yet). Another tree has a spiny toxic sap that causes severe itching for several days, and potential blindness if it gets in your eyes. Otherwise, many flowering trees and bushes, and lots of cactus. Once at the top, the views around the island were beautiful.

Our next stop was at the harbor at Ponce. We rented a car for touring Ponce and the trip next day back to San Juan. Coincidentally, we arrived in the harbor for "the spring college sports events." 30,000 college students from all over Puerto Rico come to town. It is equivalent to spring break in the US. We visited an excellent art museum in Ponce with original paintings from all over the world dating back several hundred years. We had dinner at the local mall (very nice) at what may have been the nicest restaurant in Ponce - the Sizzler. Everyone got a protein fix. We got back to the boat, which was in the harbor alongside the "boardwalk" and the Yacht Club. The boardwalk is a nice development by the city with bars, etc. We were "gently" serenaded by Marilyn Manson "occult" music until 3 in the morning. It was a tradeoff between leaving the hatches open to maintain the pleasant evening breeze, or closing the hatches to turn down the volume.

The next morning all seven of us were off to San Juan across island in the minivan. We arrived in mid-morning and toured old San Juan, a very historical area. After Columbus discovered the New World, Spain mined the New World for silver and gold, and shipped the riches to Spain via Spanish galleons. Of course, why should Spain have it all? England, France, Portugal and other pirates tried to dislodge (generally unsuccessfully) Spain for the next 400 years. Spain built about 10 strategic fortresses in the Caribbean including El Morro at the entrance to the excellent bay at San Juan. Nice informative museum-where did you think I got all of this information? In 1898 with the Spanish-American war, the U.S. had the firepower from battleships to suppress El Morro and cause the Spanish to surrender. Hence, Puerto Rico is a U.S. territory with U.S. currency but Spanish as the primary language. The biggest industries now are cruise ships and the turistas. We got a good lead from the clerk at our hotel and had lunch at El Jbardo restaurant, a great "local" establishment with excellent local dishes. We all tried conch salad (excellent) and other local cuisine. Great chocolate ice cream in large cocoa shells for dessert.

As I said earlier, the Rinks were great hosts and we had a great time. Their 40-foot sailboat is very nice with great woodwork. It has all (well, maybe some) of the amenities of home. Nice woodwork, refrigerator, stove (stabilized to offset boat rocking), sinks, showers, beds, heads, etc. Oh, it also has sails and a motor for no-wind days (which we rarely saw). The first lesson, of course, was operation of the head. No holding tanks-straight to the sea-just like whales, porpoises, and other mammals.

Of course, all of the Rinks are thoroughly suntanned. Phil is the free spirit entrepreneur teaching the family the importance of togetherness, tolerance, and family democracy (for the most part). Nancy is the fish out of water (when she is out of the water, otherwise she is just a fish), inventor of new adult beverages, and good with all of the sailing and anchor functions. Lindsay says she is really nice-and we all agree. Lena provided the saxophone serenade on the fantail of the boat, misses soccer, and does great paintings on the boat. Pender is the dinghy skipper, and has read every book on the boat-almost as many as the Library of Congress. He identifies nautical flags on boats and fighter jets on sight (many around Puerto Rico).

In any event, we had a great time with no seasickness. Good friends, good conversation, good weather, great sunrises and sunsets, and no stresses of "industrialized" life. Overall, a great vacation. We went to visit them because of the open invitation they offered on one of their earlier blanket emails. So, I assume I'm not out of bounds to tell you that you don't have much time to visit them before hurricane season starts in June. You won't regret it.

From: Phil, Nancy, Lena and Pender
To: Mermaid Distribution
Email Sent: April 25, 2002

Hello, everyone!

Wow! We've had a big few days. After sending the last email, we went to sleep and slept the sleep of the dead for about 12 hours. We did not drag anchor at all. We left early the next day and sailed the 20 miles west to West Caicos, where we tied up to a dive boat mooring buoy and had a nice dinner. After dinner we checked the wind and wave forecast and decided to quickly move on, since the current good weather was not scheduled to last.

We sailed all that night, the next day, and the next night through beautiful, although light, sailing conditions. The moon was out for most of both nights, and there were only puffy clouds in the sky. We saw the Milky Way like I haven't seen since New Mexico, and saw the Southern Cross. Both nights we had a flying fish land on deck right at about 9:30. Nancy and I took turns sleeping on the cockpit floor and actually getting some rest. It was really a beautiful trip. I found that the key to night sailing is that you must be optimistic. There is very little that you can do about anything, and if you worry too much you can't sleep and you get really tired. Of course, it's much easier to be optimistic if you aren't surrounded by lightning storms.

Anyway, after calling Bahamian customs three times on the satellite phone, we were directed to San Salvador Island to clear into customs. San Salvador is out, way out, in the northeastern part of the Bahamas. There is no way in the world that we would have gone there unless we were told to go. We planned to sail there, check in to customs, get some fuel, and get out before the coming bad weather hit. However, Alex at the dive shop, who is also the chauffeur to the customs office at the airport, assured us that (a) we could anchor safely on the island even if a swell came up, and (b) the diving there was the best in the Bahamas.

So we stayed, and we dove (dived) (went diving).

San Salvador sits on a shelf that slopes from the beach to about 40 feet, then drops off to 12,500 feet. We anchored in front of the little town, and after a small breakfast in the morning (Wednesday) Nancy and I kissed the kids goodbye, told them to get their homework done, and went diving. We tied the dinghy to a dive boat mooring in front of the marina and dropped over the side. Nancy had heard rumors about sharks, so she carried a five-foot sharp stick for protection. After dropping to the bottom, we swam to the drop-off and dropped off. Nancy was to my left, headed up current. I saw a six-foot black-tip reef shark to my right headed down current. I didn't see any need to tell Nancy. Five minutes later, I was taking pictures of the huge number of huge fish, and Nancy tapped me on the shoulder and pointed down current. Two hammerhead sharks, six and eight feet long, had swum directly over our heads and on down the reef. Nancy said she could see the eye of the larger one looking back at her. We saw some really cool fish, too, and a turtle posed for pictures.

Now for the weird part. Despite the fact that we were now positive that the ocean was full of large and potentially deadly creatures, we got the tanks filled and went diving again that afternoon. We saw another black-tip reef shark, and some more extremely cool fish. This is a great dive island. A black tip reef shark is like a prototype shark that you see in all the horror novels. Hammerheads are in the top 10 lethal shark list along with Makos, tigers, great whites, and like that.

San Salvador was supposedly named by Christopher Columbus. Supposedly he anchored there first, went ashore and traded with the Indians. The next day, a front came in and made the harbor really rolly, so he sailed 30 miles in big seas to Rum Cay, where he threaded his way into a treacherous anchorage and anchored out of the swell and settled in for a week or so of Bahamian beaching. No, sorry, that was us. CC stayed for a while in San Salvador, then sailed to Rum Cay. No word on why. Actually, CC probably went somewhere else, but I'll let you argue with the Chamber of Commerce.

On the sail from San Salvador we hooked a very large bull dolphin (mahi-mahi or dorado). Thankfully, he threw the hook, because he would have been at least 50 pounds. These fish are incredible; they can swim about 30 or 40 miles per hour for short times, and jump 5-6 feet in the air. We had this guy on long enough to get a good look at him. Then he gave our lure back. Phew. Lena made the lure. You'll be able to place orders on Doradokillerluresbylena.com.

Lena and Pender will probably finish school within two weeks, more or less. The Bahamas are great so far, and we'll do just fine here for our last five weeks.

Hope everyone is having a great spring!

Phil, Nancy, Lena and Pender

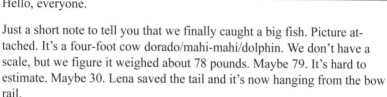

From: Phil, Nancy, Lena and Pender
To: Mermaid Distribution
Email Sent: April 29,2002

Hello, everyone.

Just a short note to tell you that we finally caught a big fish. Picture attached. It's a four-foot cow dorado/mahi-mahi/dolphin. We don't have a scale, but we figure it weighed about 78 pounds. Maybe 79. It's hard to estimate. Maybe 30. Lena saved the tail and it's now hanging from the bow rail.

We reeled this thing in on 20-pound line and a garage sale rod and reel, which was pretty cool, then squirted 12 ounces of Bombay Sapphire Gin into its gills and mouth to subdue it before we brought it onboard. That's Bombay Sapphire Gin, the choice of world-class spies and fishermen everywhere.

We are at Conception Island in the Bahamas. Very nice. White sand and crystal clear water, just like in the brochures. Hopefully we'll be here for a while.

Have a great spring. Have the
daffodils bloomed yet?

Adios

Phil, Nancy, Lena and Pender

P.S. Next time we'll have pictures of
the people you really want to see.

Phil with Dorado, Bahamas

Food

The biggest single disappointment of the trip was that we couldn't catch our dinner more often. We caught very few fish until we got to the Bahamas. We knew that we wouldn't eat any reef fish, because of concerns over ciguatera, but we were very surprised when we didn't catch many fish between islands, either.

We trailed fishing lures on every passage, but got very few bites. On one passage, the ill-fated upwind beat from Nevis to Antigua, we actually hooked three large fish but we never saw any of them. On most passages we didn't hook anything, or we would catch a small barracuda as we left the island reefs. We didn't eat any barracuda.

The fish we did catch made for some of our best meals of the trip. We caught a few tuna-type fish and had grilled tuna steaks that looked and tasted similar to extremely high-end steaks. In the Bahamas we caught three Dorado. The white meat fillets from these beautiful fish fed us for over three straight weeks and we never did get tired of it. When we ran out of fish recipes we started using our chicken recipes. The meat grilled, fried, and deep fried equally well, and took spices beautifully. Our favorites were grilled teriyaki fillet with a rice bed, and fish tacos with corn tortillas.

We ate well, in modified French style – lots of rice, potatoes or pasta, and a small portion of meat with every meal. We usually had only canned vegetables, but we ate them often. We cooked on a double-burner propane stove in the cabin or a propane barbecue on the stern rail. The cabin stove also had an oven that we almost never used. We tried using a pressure cooker early in the trip, having heard all the stories about how much time and gas they save, but we found it easier to cook in conventional ways. Our propane tanks seemed to last forever, and refilling was never a problem. Propane is not generally available in the French islands, however.

Although we were disappointed over not having freshly caught fish, we were completely delighted by the taste of fresh ripe black pineapple. We will never want to settle for pineapple from a can after eating those sweet juicy slices. The black pineapples are smaller than we are used to but their rich, round, full taste cannot be adequately described.

The local "dessert" bananas were also a treat. They were small and firm but very sweet and tasty. We also tried plantains. These relatives to the banana are cooked and eaten like potatoes. We found them an acquired taste that we never aquired and stuck with more familiar potatoes and rice.

Most towns had an open market where we bought fresh fruit and vegetables. Shopping for food in the islands was usually easy and, except in the Bahamas, there was plenty to choose from. Meat was usually frozen and in smaller portions, which fit in well with our boat diet. We bought ultra-pasteurized milk and used it for everything. It stores in boxes and doesn't need refrigeration until it's opened. It's best to plan on not buying any provisions in the Bahamas. They don't have much to sell and what they have is outrageously expensive. Some islands were even out of diesel fuel.

Cleanliness is a big deal when buying and storing food. We managed to keep Mermaid completely cockroach free, but it was a lot of work. We saw more than a few boats that were infested with ants or cockroaches. We never let fresh fruits or food packaging past the transom until it had been thoroughly inspected, cleaned, and/or discarded. Shopping meant two dinghy trips to shore: one to buy the food, and one to take the packaging to the trash container. All fresh fruits and vegetables were dipped into the salt water to chase the cockroaches off, then rinsed in fresh water and dried on deck. We stored most fruit in bags hanging off the stern rail to keep the bugs downwind and as far from the cabin as possible.

In the French islands we were happy to find freshly baked bread in almost every port. We were surprised at how good this bread is, and we haven't found anything similar since we've been home. We usually made at least one trip per day for bread, and we had to buy at least two baguettes: one for the boat and one to eat on the way back to the boat. The bread went stale quickly, so you needed to shop often and couldn't stock up for trips. The Bahamian sweet bread was also fantastic.

On most islands we would walk to the market or grocery store from the anchorage. On a few islands we needed to take a "dollar" bus. These privately run vans run on set routes. You pay when you get off, and the drivers (and the passengers) were often very helpful. On Marie Gallant in Guadeloupe, one driver walked three blocks with me to find someone who could give me directions in English. A few stores had free cabs to take you back to your dinghy when you finished shopping. Our worst experience shopping was in Fajardo on the northeast corner of Puerto Rico. After taking a cab to a nearby town, we used an Internet café and went grocery shopping. It then took us two hours to get a cab to take us back. Apparently most of the cabs stopped running about 30 minutes before we stopped shopping at five in the afternoon.

Of course, it's crucial to stow food according to a plan and a map, and for one person to be in charge of where food is stored. On Mermaid, most of the food was stored under the floor and under the seats around the dinner table, so we didn't want to have to sort around when preparing a meal. We made a map of all of the storage areas on the boat and stowed everything according to the map. If something was stored casually, it was often lost for good.

From: Phil, Nancy, Lena and Pender
To: Mermaid Distribution
Email Sent: May 6, 2002

Hello, everybody!

Mermaid has left the tropics. We left Georgetown, Bahamas at about 10 a.m. and headed north. We are now anchored at Rat Cay, which is our first experience with the shallow Bahama shoals. We left perfectly good, deep water, snuck between a couple of rocks, and found ourselves in a narrow, shallow channel between two extraordinarily shallow banks. We followed the shallow river to a calm place to anchor by using the following rules:

Dark blue=deep,
Slightly lighter dark blue=not so deep,
Slightly dark light blue=probably not deep enough,
Light blue=not deep enough,
Very slightly blue white=waist deep,
Green, with blue tones=we don't know yet, but nice to look at,
Yellow, with blue tones=shallower than green with blue tones, probably too shallow.

In places the shallow water is as warm as a swimming pool, and just as clear. It's really amazing. But, it's still less than 300 yards to very deep ocean water and the big toothy fish that swim there, so we look around a lot while snorkeling. We also clean fish while we're still sailing, not at anchor. Yesterday evening we had a four-foot barracuda and two three-foot remoras (shark suckers) swimming under the boat while we were cleaning the supper dishes with the sink draining into the ocean.

We spent a great week at Conception Island, mostly sitting around, doing very little. We caught two more Dorado on the trip from Conception to Georgetown. Nancy reeled one in. Both were caught on a Yo-Zuri 5" orange/white with a clear lip. Both were about 20 pounds, and we now have a freezer full of fish. We started making fish tacos. The recipe is: fish, half inch cubed and fried without breading; cheese; tomatoes; ranch dressing, maybe a little hot sauce, all in a fried corn tortilla. Very tasty. We could use some more Dorado recipes. Besides the tacos, we've made hash, BBQ, teriyaki BBQ, fried with garlic and brown sugar, and fried with pesto. We're not tired of it yet.

The kids are wrapping up their schoolwork and have mostly math left to do. On a related subject, beer is $40 per case here in the Bahamas. We have less than a case left, and have started to ration beer and gradually change over to rum drinks. If we run out of beer before Lena runs out of algebra, we may be in trouble.

We met a boat from Maine with two kids. They are just starting south on a one-year trip. They are part owners of a fishing fleet in Maine that includes the *Hannah Boden*, from "The Perfect Storm." The boat is now converted and is fishing red crab instead of swordfish. They used to fish crab in Alaska near where some of Nancy's family fish, and they just bought a fishing boat named *Camano*, which is our homeport. They have two boys, and their youngest one is roughly the same age as Pender and is just as involved with Lego's and fantasy stories and drawing. He and Pender had a great few days together.

We are continuing North and will be in Nassau on Memorial Day, then over to Ft. Lauderdale or Palm Beach. Still no idea what we'll do then. We tried to use the Internet in Georgetown, but BATELCO, which is the Bahama phone system, could maintain a phone connection for only five minutes at a time. Since we were paying $30/hour to use the terminal, whether the system was connected to the Internet or not, we quit and went back to the boat. Apparently that is typical for phone service in the Bahamas.

The picture was taken on Conception Island. The water in the background is about 15 feet deep, and the shallow area extends for about five miles.

Adios:

Phil, Nancy, Lena and Pender

Pender, Phil, Nancy and
Lena at Conception Island,
Bahamas

Risk

While we were planning the trip and since we returned, many people have told us that they admire our courage. Nancy and I have never really understood what these people mean. Perhaps they are politely trying to tell Nancy and me that we should be jailed rather than allowed to risk our children and ourselves in a foolhardy rush to death. Perhaps they are admiring our steadfast commitment to our children's growth, recognizing that we would go to any extreme to provide our children with the best possible environment from which we can launch our multigenerational effort to achieve total global domination. Perhaps they wish they could make the same trip, but feel that circumstances prevent them from following.

Regardless, we answer them the same way: We had to go.

We saw a developing deficit in our children's education, so we had no choice but to do whatever we could to improve their basic knowlege of Math and English.

We saw that Lena and Pender were about to leave childhood for the hell of Middle School and the potential anarchy of High School. We wanted to make sure that they had the emotional and scholastic tools they needed to survive and flourish.

We knew that our kids would face problems in the next few years that they would not be able to solve by themselves or with the help of their friends. We wanted to make sure that they knew that they could count on Nancy and me, even though we are an opinionated old couple that spends way too much time telling them what to do.

Our kids needed to know that we loved them unconditionally and that they are our first priority, even in difficult circumstances. They also needed to know that their parents were at least marginally competent when real problems need solving.

Nancy and I needed a central project to share. We had worked together to build a successful business, and our relationship flourished with the constant communication and shared goals. Since selling the business, we missed the interaction and wanted to re-invigorate our marriage.

We could have met all these challenges individually. We really didn't need a BIG project. But we had the opportunity to take a big trip, to meet and overcome really big problems together. Once we saw that a boat trip to the Caribbean met most of our families needs, how could we not go? As far as we were concerned, the greatest risk would have been to stay home.

"No, no", our now bleary-eyed friends say, "that's not what I meant. I mean, you don't know how to sail! Won't it be scary out in the open ocean?"

Oh. Well, if you've been around boats long enough, you know that there are lots and lots of incredibly incompetent boaters (luckily, very few of them will read this book and feel insulted). Very few of these unqualified captains and their hapless crew are killed. Most of them motor and sail and motorsail on their merry way, oblivious to the potential dangers they leave in their wake.

Nancy and I knew that we would read and study every possible resource. We would practice until we learned the skills required. We would seek out and follow, or at least address, the advice of experts and those who have gone before us. We would also reduce risk whenever we could by taking our time and staying informed about the weather and port conditions on our current and surrounding islands. We also commited to spending the money required to keep the boat seaworthy, fixing problems as they occured and maintaining systems to keep them working properly.

"Yeah, fine. But, really, weren't you scared?"

We were scared a lot of the time, and sometimes petrified. We just kept going.

From: Phil, Nancy, Lena and Pender
To: Mermaid Distribution
Email Sent: May 12, 2002

Happy Mother's Day all you mothers out there!

I think you know who you are.

We are at Big Majors Spot in the Exumas in the Bahamas. Big Majors is right next to Thunderball Cove, which was featured in the major motion pictures "Thunderball" and "Splash." I guess we'll have to go see it, although there was a line to go snorkeling there. A line. Of people. Waiting to go snorkeling. Maybe we won't go. Big Majors Spot is famous on its own, however. We are anchored directly in front of a small, nondescript beach. Actually, anywhere else it would be a beautiful beach, but around here it's nothing special. Anyway, people boat into the beach, then sit in their dinghies 10-15 feet offshore and wait. They don't wait long, then four little piggies and their big pink mom swim out to them and beg for food. Wow. And, there's no line.

We have collected a few snail shells on the boat. Each of them was cleaned when we collected them, but inevitably there was a small piece of meat left in each of them. I think you all can imagine what that means. Fortunately, at anchor the bow of the boat always points into the wind, so we just put the shells at the stern. We had the great idea of leaving the shells on the bottom for a while, letting the marine organisms clean them out. A hermit crab walked off with one of the shells, leaving us with a nasty broken mess of a smaller shell. Lost a shell, got a story. Seems fair.

We are broken down in Paradise. It could be worse. We motored and sailed north about 15 miles this morning to get into this more sheltered anchorage. Big southeasterly winds due tomorrow. We sailed at seven and a half knots in 12 feet of water. Anyway, our standard practice for anchoring is to motor into the anchorage, pick out a spot, stop the boat, lower the anchor, then back down hard on the anchor to "set" it into the sandy bottom. This morning we motored into the anchorage, stopped the boat, and lowered the anchor. When I put the engine control lever into reverse, nothing happened. The cable that runs from the control lever to the engine throttle had chosen that exact moment to break, leaving us no way to power the engine above idle. As far as breakdowns go, it's a medium problem. The part has to be ordered and sometimes it's hard to make sure you get the right pieces.

However, it happened after we anchored, at a spot with good communication and regular air service, as well as a nearby marina with a Fort Lauderdale branch that will trans-ship the part for $1 per pound (with two flights per week!). The lady who is watching our house manages a West Marine store, so we're pretty likely to get the right part (thanks, Nancy). So we're here for a week or so. Pretty lucky breakdown, if you ask me.

We also discovered a huge group of American boats. I think we've discovered how far south people from Florida usually go on vacation. It will probably be more crowded from here on out. We've had to turn off the radio because the Americans spend so much time talking to each other about nothing.

On a tip from some friends, we saw a great cave on a small island. The cave had ponds of water, stalactites, stalagmites, columns, water pools, and bats. Pretty cool, and no lines. In fact, no one else in sight. Literally.

Yesterday we went to an island called Little Farmers Cay. It's mostly populated by the family of the original ex-slave settlers. We met a man who opened up his very nice restaurant/bar for us. He had lived for 10 years in, among other places, Libya. We talked politics and economics. He and I had a great conversation and discussion, although we agreed on very little. It was refreshing. Anyway, the really cool thing is he was wearing a "Ballard, Washington" T-shirt. Ballard is the part of Seattle where Nancy was born and raised. Ballard is not very big, and we didn't even know they had T-shirts.

We went walking on a beautiful white sand island five days ago. It's only an island at low tide, and it's called a sand bore. We walked for over two miles and didn't see any people anywhere. The nearest boats were many miles away. Two days later we saw three eight-foot spotted eagle rays flying in formation. Spectacular.

The kids are making stop-action video movies with the digital camera and Lego pieces. I predict this will be the next great thing. They just shoot a bunch of frames, then put them into the picture program and run a "slide show" really fast. Cost=0.

A quick squall just moved through. Lena put a glass on the deck halfway through and got an inch and a half of water in ten minutes. That, and a similar storm two nights ago, are the first rain here of the year. The cisterns need the rain.

Bye for now. We'll be home soon. In the meantime, we'll be here.

From: Phil, Nancy, Lena and Pender
To: Mermaid Distribution
Email Sent: May 19, 2002

Hello, everyone.

Today is our 18th wedding anniversary. We gave each other a trip to the Bahamas.

Pender and Nancy and I went snorkeling today (we are in the Bahamas Land and Sea Park, which is like Yellowstone only wetter and less green). We saw some big fish, and four lobster fighting over three hiding places. The smallest lobster was the size of a cat, and the biggest the size of a spaniel. Pender dove down to get a closer look, about 12-15 feet down. Pretty cool. There are six-foot lemon sharks swimming around the anchorage. We will snorkel with them this evening. Maybe.

We got our replacement throttle cable in less than a week, which is light speed in the Exumas. We replaced the cable, tested it a few times, then left early the next morning. I anticipate that the new throttle cable will provide 18% better fuel mileage and a 13% increase in top speed. As we left the anchorage, we noticed that the engine-driven refrigerator kept blowing a circuit breaker. Sure enough, the electro-magnetic clutch was burned out. We now have an icebox. We have two more days of refrigerated food, then we move to the canned hams. Also, no more cold beer. Pender says the boat must know the trip is about over. Three days ago we met another family just starting out on a trip like this. We talked about looking for worms and bugs in the food and cardboard you bring aboard. I made a joke about looking out for the little tiny worms that eat into the fiberglass hull. We all laughed, but I didn't sleep well that night.

So we have a plan. We have reserved a truck to haul the boat to Seattle. He will arrive in Seattle the week before the Fourth of July. We will get to Ft. Lauderdale on June 1st or so, get the boat ready, buy a 1998 blue Volvo station wagon (with roof rack) (maybe silver), then drive to Seattle. We will definitely probably go home through New Mexico, stopping in as many places as we can, then up through Colorado and/or Utah, then etc. Driving home in a new car on interstate highways should be real interesting after spending seven months with no roads driving our house around at six miles per hour. We will arrive in Washington no later than the day before the boat does. We will probably stay downtown on the boat until the end of June.

Lena finished school today. Pender has one or two more days to go. They still have some five-paragraph essays to write. The Bahamas rainy season starts in two weeks. It's ramping into it right now. Rain doesn't bother us at all, but the wind "clocks" when a front goes though. That means that the wind blows from a different direction, making it difficult to find a calm anchorage.

We are looking at staying at three islands in the next week: Norman's Cay was run as a smuggling center by a Colombian drug lord in the 1980s (remember "Miami Vice" and "Blow"?); Highborne Cay has great snorkeling; and Allen Cay has a pack of big iguanas that beg for food on the beach, and is the jumping-off place to Nassau. In Nassau, which is apparently a drug-ridden den of iniquity, we plan to go to a water amusement park called Atlantis, then to Chub Cay, Gun Cay, and then Ft. Lauderdale.

Aloha:

Phil, Nancy, Lena and Pender

From: Phil, Nancy, Lena and Pender
To: Mermaid Distribution
Email Sent: May 28, 2002

Hello, all!

We are securely anchored at the western end of New Providence in the Bahamas. It took us five times to find some ground that would hold the anchor. We are in seven and a half feet of water, and our boat draws six feet. We ended up anchoring about 100 feet from the only other boat in the harbor. The harbor is about one mile across.

We've had some emails about the weather, so I'll discuss it a little bit. The entire western Caribbean, from Jamaica to the northern Bahamas, is covered with a "trough", or low-pressure area, combined with one or more low-pressure cells. It has been this way for more than a week. The trough could potentially produce hurricanes, which is why it's apparently on the national news, but the sea surface temperatures are much too low and the upper level winds are much too high to allow a hurricane to form in the foreseeable future.

Nonetheless, we have spent the last week or so surrounded by thunder-storms. We didn't actually end up in one until yesterday, while we were docking at Atlantis. Atlantis is a very nice resort here in Nassau. It has the largest aquarium in the world, with manta rays, hammerheads, and basically all forms of tropical fish except flying fish, ballyhoo, marlin and sailfish. It also has a good-size water park with slides and pools. Everyone should go. Anyway, while we were docking at Atlantis, the dark swirling clouds overhead finally delivered what they promised and lighting struck three times within 500 yards. The dock boy, helping us with our lines, tied off the bow line, smiled, and waved goodbye as he drove off in his golf cart. I don't blame him. We got the boat tied off well enough, then went below and huddled as far from the mast and stays as possible.

The thunderstorms here in the past few days, and forecast for the next few days, are as bad as any I've seen in New Mexico summers. The big differ-ence is that we are sitting in a big piece of Tupperware with a lightning rod stuck in the top, and we need to move in and among the thunderstorms to get out of here. I'm sure we'll be fine, and the experienced sailors from this area are probably disappointed in our lack of fortitude, but the weather has definitely added to the stress level on Mermaid. In addition, we seem to be losing our tans.

On the good side, the winds are very low right now, and should stay that way for a week. In the next few days, we plan to motor through fairly calm water 180 miles though the Gulf Stream to Ft. Lauderdale. After importing the boat, finding someone we can trust to load her on a truck, and visiting some friends in Florida, we will go shopping for that low mileage blue Volvo station wagon and head out on the highway. Lena saw a TV ad for South Florida dealer incentives on Dodge minivans. If we drive up to your house in a Dodge minivan, please shoot us immediately. Neither Nancy nor I feel ready for a minivan.

We found a scale at the resort and weighed in. Nancy now weighs 108 pounds. Pender is openly calling her a hottie. The rest of us agree. She was easily the hottest babe at the resort, including the surgically altered borg-babes. There is a small chance that the scale was not working very well. It showed me weighing less than when I graduated from high school, and Pender weighs less than any dog we've ever owned.

We are all definitely ready to come home. Today is probably our last chance to go snorkeling, and we all pass. The dinghy is on deck with a huge crack in the bottom. The refrigeration still doesn't work, but we got 35 pounds of ice at Atlantis so we have cold beer. There's probably some more stuff wrong, but I don't want to think about it and you don't want to hear about it. Mostly the kids talk about the movies they want to see.

Lena made a great art project to track the trip. She used construction paper to make a chain that runs partly around the cabin ceiling. Each link is an island that we have stayed at. There are links hanging from the chain to show the boats that we have met, and there is a second set of hanging links to show the fish we've caught. I assume that the Smithsonian will want the chain when we get home.

We'll send out a message after we get settled in Ft. Lauderdale. Don't worry if it takes a while. Plans change, things happen.

Nancy and Pender went snorkeling two nights ago. They saw a small spotted eagle ray swim by, trailing two small shark suckers (like remoras-fish that have suction cups on their heads to stick to larger fish for a free ride). Nancy and Pender swam toward the ray, and one of the 8 inch long shark-suckers peeled off of the ray and tried to stick to Pender and/or Nancy. You could hear them squeal across the harbor as they swam back to the boat. The shark sucker didn't give up until they got out of the water. It's not uncommon for a small fish to swim with you, sticking within two or three inches of you no matter what you do, but this is the first time one tried to stick with a suction cup. We checked Pender and Nancy for hickeys, but found none.

Aloha:

Phil, Nancy, Lena and Pender Rink

Little Tiny Fish

True beauty often comes in small, unexpected packages. While snorkeling in Les Saintes in Guadeloupe early in the trip, a small shiny fish followed Pender and swam wherever he did. It stayed right next to his navel when he dove, while he swam on the surface, even when he played in the shallows near the beach. It stayed with him for about an hour before it disappeared, probably to startle another tourist.

We saw these fish occasionally through-out the trip. Usually they didn't stay for long.

Lena didn't like to snorkel as much as Pender, so she hadn't seen them until we anchored at Conception Island in the Bahamas during May. We had three shiny little coins stay in the shadow of the boat all day. They would "attach" to us when we jumped in, follow as we swam and snorkeled, then hover near the swim ladder when we left the water.

We never did see these fish in a guidebook.

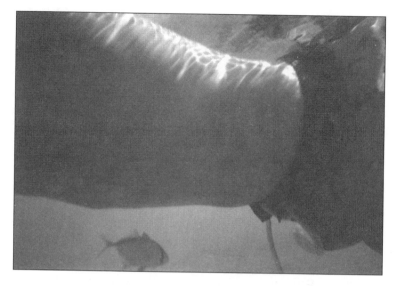

A Boy and his Fish

Lena and Friend

Our Favorite Places

Our favorite beach was Grand Anse on Guadeloupe. All the French beaches were great, but the family atmosphere and the mild but exciting surf here were perfect.

Our favorite restaurant was L'Mer in Deshaise on Guadeloupe. We didn't speak French and the waiter didn't speak English. We had him choose four different items for us and they were all very, very good. We left completely satisfied, but not stuffed.

Our favorite area was the Bahamas. Despite (or, maybe because of) the lack of infrastructure, the Bahamas are largely unspoiled and pristine. The Bahamas are approximately as large as the Caribbean chain from Puerto Rico to Trinidad. There's a lot of area to cover, and not much land. The great fishing was a bonus.

We were all very surprised at how much we like the French islands. True, the beaches are topless, which is great. But the beaches were also very family oriented. There weren't any gangs of teenagers roving the beaches. There wasn't any preening or posing. There were low-key, good-natured vendors selling donuts and bread treats, there were the Beach Ladies selling swim suits, and the sand always made perfect castles. The French towns, although occasionally poor and dirty, were always filled with good cheer and smiling faces. Of course, the food and bread were as great as you expect.

Contrasting with the French Islands was Puerto Rico. We happened to arrive during the spring student festival thing. Ponce, where we anchored, was apparently party/war zone central (depending on if you were a "student" or a police officer). The woman that rented us a car warned us to make sure to find a locked parking lot. Businesses in San Juan were boarding up their windows in preparation for the festivities. Armed guards and heavily armed soldiers were everywhere. We left Ponce after one night and moved to a quieter cove to the west. By dawn that cove was under siege as well. The five heavily armed policemen who circled our anchored boat all night said that it was "just kids having fun." Ironically, Puerto Rico was the most beautiful area we saw on the trip, both below and above the water. It was our least favorite island.

Our favorite fort was Brimstone Hill on St. Kitts. It's restored, in great shape, and not at all crowded. You need to take a cab to get there, but the driver will also be your tour guide. See the batik factory and gardens on the way. All of the forts we visited in the Caribbean were worth the visit. Some were restored, and some were just flat spots on the tops of hills. There was not much historical information at any of the Forts by American standards, and it would pay to do a little historical research before making the trip. We did buy locally published books at several museums that gave us great perspective on the history of the area.

I read James Michener's "Carribean" before we left home. The 1989 book is a fictionalized history of the entire area. Despite its simplifications and omissions (after all, it's only 800 pages in paperback), it gave a great overview of the area and provided a basic context for the trip.

It was hard for us to feel comfortable about some of the politics and race relations in the area. On most islands in the Antilles, white ex-pats now living in the Caribbean are called "locals" and the black ex-slaves are called "natives." We didn't meet a single black ex-pat. There is typically a large economic and educational gap between these two groups, although that gap is narrowing quickly on many islands. The French islands in particular have one language (on many English speaking islands the "natives" speak a compressed, faster English that we found almost impossible to understand) and a more egalitarian society. Despite all this, we never experienced or witnessed any racial tension or hostility on any island. On Nevis and St. Kitts, which are almost entirely black, people spoke a smooth, cultured form of English that was like music.

The racial disparities seem to be clearing rapidly, however. Most stores, even those with white "local" owners, are staffed and managed by blacks. The store and business managers we spoke to were working hard to improve schooling and opportunities, and the situation will be much improved within a generation as the area builds a steady economy and the business employees and managers start their own businesses.

The general atmosphere in most of the islands, especially in the Antilles and the outer islands of the Bahamas, was that of a farming or old-time western U.S. community. People were gracious and generous, tolerant yet wary of strangers, and quick to find joy in normal life. It helped to ride the local "dollar" buses. On these cramped, loud, busy buses you get more of a connection with the local lifestyle.

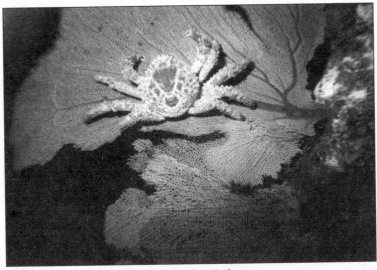

Crab on Seafan, Bahamas

From: Phil, Nancy, Lena and Pender
To: Mermaid Distribution
Email Sent: May 31, 2002

Well, we went out with a bang, and a crash, and a screech. Luckily none of those noises involved our boat.

Two nights ago we thought we might press on through to Ft. Lauderdale from the Bahama Banks. We thought the thunderstorm between us and Florida was moving west as fast as we were, so we would follow it right into the good old U.S.A. Unfortunately, it stopped, so we did too. We anchored on the bank in 16 feet of water, 15 miles from any land. It was weird, but fairly calm until about three in the morning when the wind came up and the water got a little bouncy. The next morning we stayed anchored until about nine, waiting for a window between thunderstorms to move west.

We ended up anchored at Gun Cay for the night. Gun Cay is a very small island about one mile long. We anchored in a small cove on the north end called Honeymoon Harbor. I have no idea how it got that name. Anyway, the anchorage filled up during the afternoon, both with boats moving west, waiting to cross the Gulf Stream, and boats moving east, waiting to cross the Great Bahama Banks. We went snorkeling in the harbor, and walked on the beaches. While we were on the beach, a catamaran (two hulled sailboat, very wide) pulled in and anchored very close to windward from us. Nancy checked his anchor as she snorkeled by and he did not have enough anchor line out to let the anchor sit flat on the ocean floor as the wind blew his boat back against the line. When the wind came up, his anchor would lift and come out of the sandy bottom, becoming a dragged weight instead of an anchor. Nancy stopped and very nicely told him that he had obviously anchored only temporarily, but if he let out more anchor line to hold better he would drift over our anchor and we would have to wake him when we left at two the next morning. The owner of the catamaran assured Nancy that he would move the boat and anchor properly if they stayed.

We believed him and went to bed early. When the alarm went off at 1:30, I looked out the window and saw the catamaran moving slowly downwind past our boat. Luckily, the wind had changed direction and he missed us. By the time I got the searchlight on and went on deck, he had drifted into a deeper part of the harbor and his anchor was completely free of the bottom. I shined our searchlight on him and blew our horn trying to wake him. The entire crew of the boat he was about to ram was awake and on deck trying to fend him off. We spent the next hour or so watching the crews of the catamaran, the rammed boat, and the friend of the rammed boat get everything straightened out. We couldn't have gotten out of the harbor if we wanted to because of the mess.

We waited another hour or so tracking the four thunderstorms we could see, trying to figure out which way they were going and how fast they were moving. Finally, we gave up and left, and actually had a very nice sail until the wind died, then we had a nice motor into Ft. Lauderdale. At one point we were motoring at about six knots in about a three-knot current for nine knots over the ground.

On our way into Ft. Lauderdale, a very large yacht (135 feet long) was traveling toward us so that we would pass port to port, each leaving the other on our left side, as is correct. Suddenly, the yacht turned sharply in front of us and passed off to our right. The kids thought he had messed up, but I explained to them that he had made the turn correctly, making a deliberate turn so there was no confusion about his intentions, and leaving us plenty of room to continue straight. We later met the captain of that boat (he is living right behind us) and he said that they were trying to go straight, but every time they used the remote steering station the yacht made a hard left turn. They almost ran aground.

We came into Ft. Lauderdale and motored up the New River to our present moorage at a place called Summerfields. For those of you who really, really like driving boats, you need to try driving a sailboat up a narrow river with a following tidal current. Because that might not be enough fun, there are lots of drawbridges that you need to ask to open before the current washes you into them. Then, you need to add some really big boats coming the other way. Now that's fun. Remember that you are driving a sailboat. That means you can't steer unless the boat is moving. None of this pulling over and waiting stuff.

Anyway, the sails are off the mast and stowed, the running rigging is off, and the boom and spinnaker poles have been removed. No real details on whether we have a truck yet to haul our boat to Seattle, but I'm sure that will work out fine. We're going car shopping tomorrow.

It's weird, but the sailing part of the trip is clearly over, like we turned a big switch. We will not sail Mermaid again. Right now, that seems OK to all of us. We look forward to getting home. Assuming everything comes together, we'll be driving home through New Mexico and Colorado so we can see family and friends. We'll have a party when we get back to the house. Probably not right after we get back. Drop in anytime. We took a few pictures.

Phil, Nancy, Lena and Pender

Customs and Immigration

I hate bureaucracy. I hate rules. I hate to be told I can't do something because it says so in the rules. I was terrified of having to go through customs and/or immigration as we traveled from island to island. Of all the things I worried about getting ready for the trip, this was the biggest non-issue. Except for one country, we had no problem with customs or immigration.

When we arrived in a new country, we made sure the boat was safely anchored and put away, then I changed into my clean white shirt and black shorts. I would take all the boat papers and our passports (which were kept in a special zip-up binder), my wallet, a pen, and my watch, and take the dinghy to shore. Sometimes Pender would dress in his "customs clothes" and go with me. We were almost always back to *Mermaid* within an hour, cleared in and ready to go. At the beginning of the trip, we were often frustrated in the French islands because we couldn't find the customs official right away. We soon learned that we didn't need to worry because we were free to check in at our earliest convenience. Usually it was most convenient when we were in the same place as the customs officials.

On our way back north up the island chain we saw the French officials at the dock in Les Saintes in Guadeloupe. I knocked on their boat, and told them that we had been there for two days but we hadn't checked in yet and could we do it now? The officer answered that they were just going to lunch, but they would be happy to check us in when they got back. I answered that we were just going hiking, but I would find them when we returned. That would be fine, have a good day. When we returned from our hike the customs boat had left. Two days later I checked into the "Douanes" office on the main island. The official said that he missed me after our hike. I said, "Yeah, the kids walk slow." He laughed, we checked in, and we were on our way.

Some of the islands, especially those with British backgrounds, had more formal and pretentious requirements. At no time were we treated badly. We did have to adjust our cruising schedules to accommodate, for instance, checkout office hours. Overall, though, it was not a problem. There are some cruisers who simply ignore the whole thing. We didn't get that relaxed.

We had done our research, and our paperwork was in order. *Mermaid* was U.S. Coast Guard Documented, we all had passports, and we carried all required radio licenses. We were always polite and never (very) impatient. We were businesslike and friendly. In one or two places (the BVI come to mind) we had to get the officials to stop fooling around in the back room and help us, but even there we were done and out the door quickly.

Returning to the U.S., however, was a nightmare. Before we left home I met with the customs official here in our hometown and described our project, including the fact that we had bought a boat and would need to import it. No, they didn't have a written pamphlet or procedure, but here's what you need to do–it's simple. Then we cleared into the U.S. Virgin Islands, our first stop in the United States. Whoops, a whole new set of rules. Then into Puerto Rico and different set of rules. Then into the United States in Fort Lauderdale. One 15-minute phone call on the satellite phone and three more 45-minute phone calls from a pay phone ("please hold, your call is important to us") later and we were told another set of rules. So, a trip to the commercial port with a handful of cash and another wait in line. "You brought cash! Who told you that? We won't take your money, you need an agent to import your boat. There's an agent in the next building." The agent was more than happy to take our money, plus his fee (which was approximately equal to the duty), to import the boat for us. It would be really easy to excuse the whole mess as fallout from the September 11 terrorism, but it was all about bureaucracy and taxes.

No one ever looked at the boat. I'm not going to give you the procedure we followed because I doubt it will help. Just pretend that you are entering a banana republic ruled by a military junta that just claimed back power from the revolutionaries and hire an agent, paying whatever he asks.

Pender driving in the Bahamas.

From: Phil, Nancy, Lena and Pender
To: Mermaid Distribution
Email Sent: June 11, 2002

Hello, all:

We've had more than one request to continue the reports until we get home, so I'm afraid that those of you who are bored with the whole thing will be bored a little longer.

Returning to the United States was every bit as painful as we anticipated. The U.S. Customs Service has no idea what they are doing. Every person we talked to told us a different thing, and we finally ended up having to use a customs broker to wade through the mess for us. In addition to our 1.5% duty on the boat, we had to pay about $1,500 in fees and bond to bring the boat into the country. The mess and confusion had nothing to do with increased security, because they had no interest in the boat or its contents, only in the paperwork and money.

The problems with customs would have made us really unhappy except we had bigger problems with the entire trucking industry. The truck that we had booked backed out on us after we arrived in Florida, and three other companies changed their quotes, increasing the prices about 30%. We finally found somebody who will haul the boat to Seattle for us, for only another $1,000 and four weeks delay.

We bought a white Mercury Sable station wagon. There are very few blue Volvo wagons available in south Florida. We found a black one that was OK, but had a few more miles than what we wanted. We like the Sable a lot.

After working furiously on the boat for six days, we finally got out of Ft. Lauderdale, drove a few miles north to Vero Beach, and met up with some friends just in time to watch the space shuttle Endeavor take off. It was amazing, even though we were two hours south of the launch site. We slept on our friends' boat that night, then got up and drove to Cape Canaveral. On the way we stopped in Cocoa Beach at the world's largest surf shop: Ron Jon's. We got Lena a new bikini for her 13th birthday and a sticker for the new car, then we drove to the Kennedy Space Center visitor center, which was great.

From there we drove to Carlsbad, NM, to see the caverns and to White Sands to see the inland beach. It was very interesting to see the geology around Carlsbad, which is exactly identical to the Bahamas. The uplifted seabed is called Karst, and is very distinctive. The formation of Carlsbad Caverns is the same as the much smaller cave we saw in the Bahamas. There were more bats in the cave in Carlsbad. We came back to the cave at dusk to watch the bats fly. The park rangers put on a nice little show to stall the crowd (maybe 100-150 people) until the bats decide to come out. Once the bats start flying, they swarm out of the cave like a whirlwind, taking over half an hour for the swarm (herd?) to leave the cave. It was really amazing.

White Sands, in southern New Mexico, is a huge area of white gypsum sand dunes. It's really beautiful, hot and bright. We got a quick tan boost and moved on. Somehow a big inland beach didn't hold the kids' attention. Go figure.

We'll spend the rest of June visiting family and friends between New Mexico and Washington, and be home the first of July. We'll write one more Mermaid report once the boat is safely in Seattle. That should be the third week in July.

Adios, amigos!

Phil, Nancy, Lena and Pender

Shipping the Boat

When we started planning the trip, we knew that we would want to ship *Mermaid* to Seattle when our trip was over because the market was so strong, and she was worth much more in the Pacific Northwest than she was in Ft. Lauderdale. By the time our trip ended, we decided that we had better ship *Mermaid* to Seattle because it looked like the market for used boats was so glutted that we may end up owning her for a long, long time. We needed to keep her where we could keep an eye on her.

For us, shipping was a nightmare that started bad but only got worse. We tried hard to do our homework, contacting many shippers before we left home to get quotes and to try to establish communication. Universally, they told us that we were starting too soon, that we should wait until we were closer to our ship date, then start working on finding a shipper.

Unfortunately, when we started looking for a shipper in April, most of the shippers were booked up and many were very difficult to work with by email. "Please call the office during business hours and we'll help you," they'd reply. "But we're at sea," we'd tell them, or, "we're in the Bahamas."

We finally found a shipper who could move our boat. He quoted a pickup date, a delivery date, and a price over the phone. I asked him if we needed a confirmation number. "No," he said, "I've got your boat name and date, which is all I need to find your quote. Just call me when you get to Ft. Lauderdale." We relaxed and finished our cruise.

When we arrived in Ft. Lauderdale, we called him. "No problem," he said, "let me check with the driver and call you back." We don't have a phone, can we call him again? "No sweat, call me tomorrow afternoon." The next afternoon we called him. "We will pick your boat up in three weeks."

"No," I said, "that's when you agreed to drop our boat in Seattle."

"Can't help you then." And he hung up. I called back. He wouldn't take our call.

Long story short, we found a shipper who would deliver our boat to Seattle. It would take only an extra month and an extra thousand dollars, but the boat would get there. We checked around, the guy was legit, so we did the deal. Packed up the boat, dropped and stowed the rig, and we were out of there. We elected to buy a car and drive home because we needed a car anyway and we could visit relatives and friends on the trip home. We had a great, leisurely drive home diagonally across the country.

The boat finally arrived in Seattle, a week later than promised. The trailer had broken down several times on the trip. I think the driver said that he blew seven tires. The trailer was completely rusted out, with fresh blue paint over the rust.

We got the keel recoated and painted, and the boat launched and rigged. Now she's for sale, waiting for the next family that needs a little beauty and adventure.

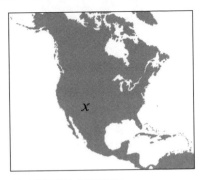

From: Phil, Nancy, Lena and Pender
To: Mermaid Distribution
Email Sent: June 11, 2002

YOU AND YOUR FAMILY AND/OR FRIEND
are invited to the first annual
RETURN TO PARADISE PARTY.
Sunday
1:00 until dark or so.
(Eat lunch before the party.)
Grill starts up at 4 p.m.
We supply burgers, hotdogs, and condiments.
You bring drinks and a salad or dessert.
Bring whatever sports equipment you want, including swimsuits if you want
to play in the pond or "Slip and Slide."
If you would like to play, please bring musical instruments.

Please, no fireworks.
The Rink House
Camano Island, WA
Go past the alpaca farm, grocery store, and golf course.
If you don't mind walking down the driveway, please park on the road.

Please RSVP to this email address. We don't have a phone yet. If you know
someone who should be invited and wasn't, please invite them and ask them
to RSVP. We won't be back in the state until July and we may not have a
phone for a while.

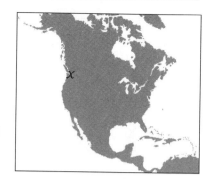

From: Phil, Nancy, Lena and Pender
To: Mermaid Distribution
Email Sent: July 12, 2002

Howdy, and we hope you are all having a great summer!

We are home and mostly moved back into our house. The woman who was staying here left everything in great condition. There was even beer in the fridge. The kids filled bags with their clothes that don't fit anymore, and we've been shopping for new shoes. Our tans have faded, although they haven't disappeared, and we are all getting dark roots in our hair.

The cars were mostly fine, although we had to put a new fuel pump in the Suburban and the batteries in the boat are shot. The Suburban also had at least two families of mice living in and around the engine. We haven't found any in the passenger compartment yet.

The yard was in great shape. As we usually do this time of year, we spent a few days pulling thistle before they bud out. We filled the old chicken coop with thistle plants. They should compost within five years. We haven't done anything with the nettles yet. Maybe next year.

To encourage ourselves to get the house put back together, we had an open house the Sunday after we got home. Even though it rained all day and we couldn't play in the yard, we had a great time and got to see a lot of our friends. The weather since then has been great, over 80 and very sunny. Almost tropical. Certainly hot enough for rum drinks.

Pender and Lena are eager to spend time with friends, and can't wait for camp at the end of this month and soccer season starting soon after. Nancy is joining a women's soccer league.

It looks like a return to the real world is inevitable. We are currently looking for project$ to work on. If anyone has any products or prototypes they want developed, please call or email at the address shown below. I promise to work as if I live in a house in the Northwest, not on a boat in the tropics. We are also putting together a video of the trip and a book. Hopefully both will be ready for the boat show season.

Thank you all very much for your support. Your emails and comments were a real part of our trip. Two frequently asked questions:

Would we do it again? Nancy and I will take another trip, once the kids are out of school. The kids can do it again when they grow up, assuming they marry well.

Would you recommend other people take the trip? There is no way we would ever talk anybody into doing this. It was more of an adventure than a vacation, and at times was very dangerous and/or uncomfortable. On the other hand, we are extremely glad we went, we all grew a lot, and as time goes on we remember the trip as more and more fun.

Please take care of each other.

Love:
Phil, Nancy, Lena and Pender Rink

The End

Reference A - Equipment List

Things we packed and brought with us:

Description	Make/Model	Comment
Nutmeg and grater		
Zipties		For sealing shipping containers.
Baja Filter	West Marine	Large Plastic
Watermaker	Village Marine Little Wonder	Worked well.
Watermaker spares and filters	Village Marine.	
BBQ	Magma Marine Kettle,	Rail mount used portable propane tanks.
Boat brush		
Playing cards		
Em. Bilge Pump	Jabsco 1750 GPH	With long hose and cig. lighter power cord.
Fish scale 5 lbs.		What were we thinking? The lures weigh 5 lbs.
Fluorescent light		Auto parts store cheapie.
Gloves, sailing	O'Brien water skiing gloves	
Hose, shower		To replace hose in aft head.
Inflator, raft		
Knife sharpener		
Light, solar	Converted yard light.	Great cockpit/anchor light.
Light, spot		12 VDC with lighter plug.
Mouth horn	"Horatio Hornblower"	
Nets, lifeline		
Offshore harnesses		
Reflector tape	Scotch-Brite tape.	Used to mark outboard and hull.
Sail tape		
Socket, lighter	Installed at helm.	
Soldering iron	Radio Shack, propane.	Also used for heat-shrink.
Tell-tells	Installed on Jib.	
Tie-downs, ratchet wire	Large capacity, 3" web.	Used to hold dinghy on foredeck.
12 VDC Ext. Cords		
Binoculars	With integral compass.	
Burglar Alarms	Never used.	
CD Player	Jensen 10-Disk.	Installed on AM/FM radio.
EPIRB	ACR Rapidfix w/GPS interface	
Helm Plotting GPS	Garmin 162	Fantastic!
EPIRB GPS	Garmin Etrex	Stored with EPIRB
Backup GPS	Garmin GPS III w/cord	
Hand-held VHF	Standard HX460S	Fantastic!
Camera strobe	Ikelite	
Underwater film		
Camera housing	Ikelite Aqua-Shot	Uses disposable cameras.
Inverter, 1000W	Cheap	
Inverter, 140W	Cheap	
Labelmaker		
Pillowcases		
Rain ponchos (3)		
SSB Receiver	Si-Tex	
Weather FAX software		Came with SSB receiver.

Reference A - Equipment List

Things we packed and brought with us:

Description	Make/Model	Comment
Towels		
Voltmeters		
Underwater Vid Cam-Fisheye 200C		
Fishing lures		
Fishing reel		
Flags, USA		
Flashlights		
Hacksaw		
Drill and charger	Makita cordless	
Music CD's		
SCUBA regulators		
Scissors		
Stapler and staples		
Vacuum gauge	For fuel filter (never installed)	
Yacht club burgee		
Boat books		
Charts, flat		
Guide books		
Kids reading books		70#
Printer cartridges		Never used.
Printer	Canon 0010X347	Never used.
School books		
Cooler bag		
School supplies		
FRS radios	Kenwood	Very nice to use ashore
Cam for Ikelite (10)	FUJI disposable cameras.	
Flute and Sax		
Binoculars (Black)		
Blank CD's (3 Pkgs)		
Laptop computer	Compaq Presario 4120	
Computer CD's		
Laptop computer	Dell Inspiron 8000	
Diskettes (20)		
Satellite phone	Iridium	Great for voice, email and Internet.
Point and Shoot	Olympus weatherproof	
Digital camcorder	Sony D8 DCR-TRV730	Fantastic
Hi8 camcorder	Sony Hi8 CCD-TRV62	Backup
Digital still camera	Sony MVC-FD88	
Blank video tapes		
Sun glasses		
Transom logo	Vinyl transfer.	Could have bought in St. Maarten.
Ascender	JUMAR.	Used for climbing the mast.
Bandages, extra		
First aid kit		Offshore. No hard drugs.
Waterproof rolltop bags		
Foul weather gear, kids		
Garlic press		
Jacklines		

Reference A - Equipment List

Things we packed and brought with us:

Description	Make/Model	Comment
Life jackets		(4 inflatable)
Life jackets		(Kids)
Work and dive light	Nite Rider	
Offshore tethers		
Power Pak		Portable 12 Volt Source
Weather cloths	Made w/Sailrite materials	Cockpit sun/spray screens.
Games		
Guest book		
Lightning diss.		Homemade from unwoven 7X19 SS wire. Mounted at mast-head.
Pressure cooker		Did not used.
Tool kit		
Vacuum food packer		Used all the time.
Vacuum packer bags		
Art supplies		
Batteries & charger	Radio Shack.	Li-MH.
Bug spray		
Games		
Sunscreen		
Vacuum, 12V	Never used.	
Dive gear		
Boat stamp	Never used.	
Flags, courtesy	Homemade.	We also bought along the way.
Paddle blades		
Pushpit seats	Homemade from Starboard.	Great.
Shelves	Homemade from Starboard.	Installed in kid's hanging lockers. Really improved storage.
Skins	Whole-body swimsuits	
Snorkeling gear	US Diver for kids.	Good quality.
Tent	Never used.	
Rescue throw bag	Homemade.	
Shorty wetsuits (4)		
Chart books		
Gauze wrap		
Wet balls		Beach toys.
Breeze Booster		Hatch-mounted draft inducer.
Hammock		
Music books		
Documentation papers		
Insurance papers		
Radio license		
Learning 2000	Gateway Computers	Great computer learning programs.
Passports		
Passports, copies		
Phone and address book		
Hats		
Sandals	TEVA	Buy the best you can find.
Flashlights		
Fleece sleeping bags (2)		Worked great for the kids.

Reference A - Equipment List

Things we bought in St. Maarten:

Description	Make/Model	Comment
Life Raft	Zodiac "Open Sea" 6 Man	Valise
Spare Anchor	Fortress FX-23 with 20' chain and 200' of 5/8 Nylon	Great Anchor, kept knocked down in cockpit locker
Flares		Various SOLAS hand-held and parachute.

Reference A - Equipment List

Things that came with the Boat:

Description	Make/Model	Comment
Autopilot	Autohelm ST4000 Inboard	Great
Depth sounder	Teleflex digital	Minimal
Docklines	Lots	
Engine	Yanmar 45 HP	Great, replaced water pump
Fenders	Lots	
Dishes		
Kitchen utensils		
Pots and pans		
VHF ant.	Masthead	
Main anchor	35# plough	Great
Main anchor rode	100' 3/8 chain, 100' nylon	Great
Anchor and rode, dinghy	Grapnel, 3#	
Anchor and rode, stern	Generic 20# Danforth Type	
Dinghy	3 meter AB RIB	Old, but OK
Dinghy outboard	15 HP Mercury Sea Pro	Lower unit leaked, fixed
Dinghy gas container	6 Gal Poly	
Foul weather gear		Looked OK, but leaked
Horseshoe buoy with automatic light		
Radar reflector	Rigging mounted tube type.	
Bedding		
Propane tanks	(2) Aluminum 20#	Plenty of gas.
Refrigeration	Sanden based custom cold plate	Adequate, but troublesome.
Wind generator	Air Marine	Trouble free, low power, very loud.
Alternator	Yanmar 80A internal regulator	Marginal, 150A with external regulation would have been better.
Anchor windlass	Lofrans "Tigres"	Great, replaced worn gypsy.
Heads	PAR manual	Replaced seals, worked great.
Life jackets	Big orange cheapies	We always used inflatables.
House batteries	2 ea. group 27 lead-acid.	Replaced before trip. Barely adequate.
Engine starting battery	group 27 lead-acid.	
Bosun's chair		Used climbing gear and harness.

Reference B - Planning Calendar

Sail your own boat and plan your own trip. Read ahead.

Now:

· Watch the video: "Mermaid: Our Family in Paradise" with your family.
· Look at boats. There are lots of boats for sale in Marin, Martinique; Point a Pitre, Guadeloupe; St. Maarten; and the Virgin Islands. Look at local models, and shop on the web at www.yachtworld.com.
· Start researching insurance.
· Take the USCG or US Power Squadron safe boating class(es).
· Read: "Mermaid: Our Family in Paradise".

April:

· Make an offer on the yacht you choose, and pick out at least one back-up yacht. Use your own broker, separate from the listing broker. Check your broker's references.
· Take a sailing class.
· Check with the CDC website and start getting recommended shots.
· Read: "A Gentleman's Guide to Passages South," by Bruce Van Sant.

May:

· Have the yacht and engine surveyed, inspect the yacht and complete the purchase.
· Secure hull insurance. Investigate joining the Seven Seas Cruising Association at ssca.org.
· Check your health insurance, and look into medical evacuation services such as offered by the Diver's Alert Network (D.A.N.).
· Have the yacht delivered to St. Maarten and stored for the summer on land. There's lots of storage on Simpson Bay Lagoon.
· Arrange for any required servicing, excluding rigging.
· Have the sails repaired and order new sails if required.
· Have the yacht documented by the US Coast Guard. We used an agent suggested by our broker.
· Get catalogs from West Marine in the US and Budget Marine and Island Water World in St. Maarten.
· Go to marine garage and sidewalk sales.
· Brush up on your first-aid skills and take classes if required. Get a good medical reference book like the "DK Complete Home Medical Guide" and a full first-aid kit. Plan on being at least three days from medical help.
· Read: "The Concise Guide to Caribbean Weather," by David Jones.

Reference B - Planning Calendar

June:

·   Start buying used and discount age-appropriate books. The kids will soon be at least one grade level above their current level. You need at least 70 pounds of kid books and a few challenging adult books. You can buy and trade for best sellers at the book swaps throughout the Caribbean.

·   Research the web for current licensing requirements for U.S. yachts operated abroad.

·   Make sure everyone in the family has a valid passport.

·   Start shopping for cruising equipment and safety gear. Remember to check with suppliers in St. Maarten, which is duty free and not expensive, especially for items made in France and other EU countries (email works great).

·   Start swimming lessons.

·   Volunteer as crew in local sailing races.

·   Watch the video: "Mermaid: Our Family in Paradise" with your family again. Discuss expectations and anxieties. Give each family member a task to research and complete.

·   Read: "Cruising for Cowards," by Liza & Andy Copeland.

July:

·   Find a house sitter.

·   Order a life raft to pick up in St. Maarten.

·   Buy and register your EPIRB. The new ones with the integral GPS are amazing.

·   Read: "Caribbean," by James A. Michener.

August:

·   Buy all the cruising guides: Windward Islands; Leeward Islands; the Virgin Islands; and Explorer Charts for the Bahamas.

·   Read: "Boatowner's Mechanical and Electrical Manual," by Nigel Calder. Memorize the index.

September:

·   Meet with teachers and buy or borrow learning materials, reference books and software.

·   Start going to tanning booths and get a really good tan.

·   Read: Search the Internet for health, political, and governmental issues with your cruise.

Reference B - Planning Calendar

October:

- Buy all the supplies you couldn't find on sale or buy in St. Maarten.
- Double-check with airline for packing rules and start packing early in the month using Rubbermaid totes. Pack each to the maximum weight and attach the lids with zip ties through holes drilled in the lid flange. Pack extra zip ties in carry-on luggage in case the totes are opened at airport by security. Pack fishing poles and spears in a piece of PVC pipe.
- Make arrangements for travel to the airport. Remember that you will have lots of luggage.
- Read: "Sailing for Dummies," by JJ Isler and Peter Isler.

November:

- Travel to St. Maarten!
- Move on to your yacht.
- Rent a car for the first week to run errands.
- Visit and join the St. Maarten Yacht Club, just south of the Dutch Bridge. Go for free rum drinks every night ½ hour before the last bridge opening. Ask lots of questions, and listen to the answers. Have some dinner. Find out the schedule for the St. Maarten Yacht Club Heineken Regatta in early March.
- The first day you have the car, visit all the major food stores. Note which store carries what and buy samples of new foods or brands that you might want to buy in quantity. Buy your provisions later in the week, but while you still have the rental car.
- Install equipment and complete repairs as soon as possible.
- Double- check the weather for hurricanes, then have the boat launched and anchor in the lagoon.
- Set up your daily schedule with school first, but find lots of time for dinghy trips to the close-in beaches and a long walk (or taxi ride) to Maho beach to see the planes land and take off.
- Have the boat rigged professionally.
- Service the dinghy outboard.
- Double-check the refrigeration, charging and battery systems, and the anchor winch, and have them serviced if required.
- Practice with your GPS, calibrate your depth sounder and practice anchoring as a family.
- Pack the boat according to a "map".
- Learn the bridge schedule, and then go out day sailing. Take your time but make it back to the lagoon for the last bridge.

Reference B - Planning Calendar

November (continued):
- Pick a calm day and sail around the island.
- Listen to the cruiser net each morning at 7:30 (VHF 14).
- Listen to the weather reports on ZBVI (AM) and on the SSB receiver.
- Pick up books at the various book swaps.
- Read: Cruising guides and equipment manuals.

December:
- You're off. St. Barts is great. See if Jimmy Buffet is playing at Le Select.
- Have a great time, take your time, and watch the weather. Always sail your own boat.

March:
- Back to St. Maarten for the St. Maarten Yacht Club Heineken Regatta. You'll have the most fun if you volunteer to help.

April:
- Head for the Bahamas.

June:
- Back to the U.S.A.
- The hurricane season in the Bahamas officially starts in June, but many consider it the most beautiful time to be in the island country.
- Truck your yacht to your hometown or the best market and sell her.

Reference C - Where We Stayed

This list contains most of the anchorages we stayed in and a very short general comment for each one. Our comments are based on one trip, one time there, so don't give them any more value than they deserve. The guidebooks will have much more information on accommodations than we can provide.

Anchorage	Comment
Simpson Bay Lagoon, St. Maarten	Great place to start, great place to be. Very friendly people.
Anguilla South Coast	Peaceful, friendly. Not accessible during normal trade winds.
St. Barths	Crowded, cool, lots of naked Germans.
St. Kitts	Urban, good fort.
Nevis	Rolly anchorage, very nice feel to town.
Falmouth Harbour, Antigua	Exciting, big-time yachting.
Deep Bay, Antigua	Too much cruise ship traffic in St. John. Deep Bay was nice.
Nonsuch Bay, Antigua	Great. Just plain great. Kite surfing, snorkeling, cool.
Deshaise, Guadeloupe	Great food at L'Mer, Grand Anse beach was great. Perfect.
Pidgeon Island, Guadeloupe	Great diving, snorkeling. Nice people.
Basseterre, Guadeloupe	A city. Good fort. Great French fashions.
Pointe a Pitre, Guadeloupe	Good supplies, shallow water north of the anchorage.
St. Anne, Guadeloupe	Great beach, good town. Very rolly anchorage.
St. Pierre, Guadeloupe	Small anchorage, nice beach.
Marie Gallant, Guadeloupe	Open anchorage, very nice island with working sugar mill.
Les Saintes, Guadeloupe	Smooth and easy, great fort.
St. Pierre, Martinique	Very cool old town, lots of history.
St. Anne, Martinique	Very nice beach, nice place to hang out. Great bakery.
Spanish Town, BVI	Convienient check-in point.
Anegada, BVI	Great snorkeling, flamingos, good anchorage.

Reference C - Where We Stayed

Anchorage	Comment
Leverick Bay, BVI	Great anchorage, good buffalo wings at the old Pussers.
Bitter End YC, BVI	Movie night, sailboat rentals. Inexpensive luxury for cruisers.
Sandy Spit, BVI	Still our favorite island.
Jost Van Dyke, BVI	We sat in hammocks and talked to our friends, and our kids got us beers from the bar. Great food at Club Paradise.
The Bight, BVI	Good food and entertaining customers at the WillyT.
Great Lameshur Bay, USVI	Peaceful, nice hike.
Charlotte Amalie, USVI	Nice city, easy shopping.
Megans Bay, USVI	Great Easter party, noisy Puerto Rican boat flotilla, bossy lifeguards and boisterous crowds on the beach.
Dewey, Puerto Rico	Flamingo Beach was great, nice town.
Fajardo, Puerto Rico.	Civilization. Showers. Ice in drinks. Noise. Traffic.
Isla Mujeres, Puerto Rico	Manatees, spotted eagle rays.
Caja de Muertes	Quiet, good hiking, open anchorage.
Ponce, Puerto Rico	Hot, loud, buggy, stressful.
Old San Juan, Puerto Rico (by car)	Nice walking, forts, great lunch, lots of heavily armed guards.
Margarita Reef, Puerto Rico	Ran aground. Was helped by two very nice men.
Boqueron, Puerto Rico	Jumping-off point for the Bahamas.
French Cay, Turks and Caicos	We'll have to go back. We were tired from the trip from PR.
San Salvador, Bahamas	Surprisingly great. Fantastic diving, very friendly people.
Rum Cay, Bahamas	Peaceful, isolated.
Conception Island, Bahamas	Lots of cruisers, incredible snorkeling and exploring.
Georgetown, Bahamas	Cruisers everywhere. Friendly place.
Rat Cay, Bahamas	Great anchorage.
Big Galliot Cay, Bahamas	We walked on our own sand bore for over two miles.

Reference C - Where We Stayed

Anchorage	Comment
Little Farmers Cay, Bahamas	Very friendly people, cave on nearby island.
Big Majors Cay, Bahamas	Very friendly people, easy anchorage. Pig on beach. Thunderball grotto.
Warderick Wells, Bahamas	Bahamas Land and Sea Park. Incredible snorkeling and exploring.
Highborne Cay, Bahamas	Shell beach, nurse sharks.
Paradise Island, Bahamas	Atlantis Resort was awesome.
Honeymoon Harbor, Bahamas	Crowded anchorage waiting to cross to Fort Lauderdale.
Fort Lauderdale, FL	We were ready to be back, but what a hassle.

Reference D - Reading List

Mermaid, Our Family in Paradise (Video) ISBN 0-9727906-0-8. www.caribmermaid.com.

The Gentleman's Guide to Passsages South by Bruce Van Sant. ISBN 0-944428-31-2.

CARIBBEAN by James A. Michener. ISBN 00-449-21749-3.

The Squadron Boating Course by The United States Power Squadron. Book and Video Set. ISBN 0-688-17567-8.

Cruising for Cowards by Liza and Andy Copeland. ISBN 0-9697690-3-2.

Sailing for Dummies by JJ Isler and Peter Isler. ISBN 0-7645-5039-X.

Quick Reference Weather Forecasting by Davis Instruments, ISBN 1-892524-06-6 (Plastic Placard).

The Concise Guide to Caribbean Weather by David Jones, ISBN 0-9652476-1-9.

Boatowner's Mechanical and Electrical Manual by Nigel Calder. ISBN 0-07-009618-X.

Cruising Guide to the Leeward Islands by Chris Doyle. ISBN 0-944428-51-7 (get the current version).

Cruising Guide to the Windward Islands by Chris Doyle. ISBN 0-944428-53-3 (get the current version).

Cruising Guide to the Virgin Islands by Nancy and Simon Scott. ISBN 0-944428-52-5 (get the current version).

The Explorer Chartbook and Cruising Guide for the Exhumas and Ragged Islands of the Bahamas by Monty and Sara Lewis, Lewis Offshore Ltd; (410) 213-2725.

Fish Indentification Placards by Seahawk Press, 6840 S.W. 92 St., Miami, FL 33156.

Various guidebooks for the Bahamas by Stephen Pavlidis.

About the Author

Phil Rink was born and spent most of his pre-adult childhood and all of his adolescense in Los Alamos, New Mexico. He went to the University of New Mexico in Albuquerque, NM and was granted a BSME in 1982 on the four and a half year college program.

His first engineering job was in the Navy shipyards in Bremerton, WA, where he met Nancy. Ironically, at the time Nancy was an mechanical engineering student at UNM in Albuquerque. She and Phil had never met, although six months before then Nancy had done the two-step with Phil's best friend from college. The two-step, as most of you know, is a cowboy dance.

The shipyard did not work out for Phil, and when Nancy returned to school in the fall Phil went back with her, intending to get a graduate degree. Luckily for the academic world, Phil found an engineering job in Los Alamos before school began. That job was the first in a long string of jobs, seven in the next ten years, as Phil followed his interests and tried to avoid unintentional unemployment. Most of the jobs were for smaller companies designing and building robots, automated equipment, or doing manufacturing engineering. He has nine patents so far, and one or two in the mill.

Phil's first boating experience of note was on Lake Mead in his Dad's 14 foot Starcraft aluminum runabout with a 25 horse-power Gale outboard. Their family beat that boat to death, even skiing behind it in the cold New Mexico lakes. During college Phil had a seventeen-foot canoe stored upside down on a huge frame in living room of his apartment.

Nancy and Phil now live in a beautiful house they designed and built. It overlooks a beaver pond in northwest Washington. They continue to spend as much time with their kids as they can, working at school and coaching soccer, while they work at developing the "next great thing". At this point they have no idea what thing will be great next.

Our Family in Paradise

About the Video

While we were planning this trip, Nancy and I looked for videos that would show Lena and Pender some of the basics about living on a sailboat and cruising in tropical waters.

We didn't find one that had the pacing and visual interest to keep the kids entertained, but with enough information to help the kids form reasonable expectations about their life afloat.

We all helped collect footage during our trip, and the half-hour video we put together provides a good introduction to family life afloat. The video is all digital quality. Professional sound and editing make it pleasant to watch and exciting to discuss.

Sections of the video deal with a typical day at anchor, life on passage, our favorite things to do, and the dangers of cruising. There's just enough scenic and underwater footage to give everyone a taste of the tropics. Watch it while sitting under a heat lamp to get the full effect.

You can buy a copy of the video where you bought this book, or order directly from our website at www.caribmermaid.com.

Thanks for sharing our adventure. Start planning yours today!